I0409733

THE U.S.-SAUDI ARABIA COUNTERTERRORISM RELATIONSHIP

HEARING

BEFORE THE

SUBCOMMITTEE ON TERRORISM, NONPROLIFERATION, AND TRADE

OF THE

COMMITTEE ON FOREIGN AFFAIRS
HOUSE OF REPRESENTATIVES

ONE HUNDRED FOURTEENTH CONGRESS

SECOND SESSION

MAY 24, 2016

Serial No. 114–162

Printed for the use of the Committee on Foreign Affairs

Available via the World Wide Web: http://www.foreignaffairs.house.gov/ or
http://www.gpo.gov/fdsys/

U.S. GOVERNMENT PUBLISHING OFFICE

20–256PDF   WASHINGTON : 2016

For sale by the Superintendent of Documents, U.S. Government Publishing Office
Internet: bookstore.gpo.gov   Phone: toll free (866) 512–1800; DC area (202) 512–1800
Fax: (202) 512–2104   Mail: Stop IDCC, Washington, DC 20402–0001

COMMITTEE ON FOREIGN AFFAIRS

EDWARD R. ROYCE, California, *Chairman*

CHRISTOPHER H. SMITH, New Jersey	ELIOT L. ENGEL, New York
ILEANA ROS-LEHTINEN, Florida	BRAD SHERMAN, California
DANA ROHRABACHER, California	GREGORY W. MEEKS, New York
STEVE CHABOT, Ohio	ALBIO SIRES, New Jersey
JOE WILSON, South Carolina	GERALD E. CONNOLLY, Virginia
MICHAEL T. McCAUL, Texas	THEODORE E. DEUTCH, Florida
TED POE, Texas	BRIAN HIGGINS, New York
MATT SALMON, Arizona	KAREN BASS, California
DARRELL E. ISSA, California	WILLIAM KEATING, Massachusetts
TOM MARINO, Pennsylvania	DAVID CICILLINE, Rhode Island
JEFF DUNCAN, South Carolina	ALAN GRAYSON, Florida
MO BROOKS, Alabama	AMI BERA, California
PAUL COOK, California	ALAN S. LOWENTHAL, California
RANDY K. WEBER SR., Texas	GRACE MENG, New York
SCOTT PERRY, Pennsylvania	LOIS FRANKEL, Florida
RON DeSANTIS, Florida	TULSI GABBARD, Hawaii
MARK MEADOWS, North Carolina	JOAQUIN CASTRO, Texas
TED S. YOHO, Florida	ROBIN L. KELLY, Illinois
CURT CLAWSON, Florida	BRENDAN F. BOYLE, Pennsylvania
SCOTT DesJARLAIS, Tennessee	
REID J. RIBBLE, Wisconsin	
DAVID A. TROTT, Michigan	
LEE M. ZELDIN, New York	
DANIEL DONOVAN, New York	

AMY PORTER, *Chief of Staff*   THOMAS SHEEHY, *Staff Director*

JASON STEINBAUM, *Democratic Staff Director*

————

SUBCOMMITTEE ON TERRORISM, NONPROLIFERATION, AND TRADE

TED POE, Texas, *Chairman*

JOE WILSON, South Carolina	WILLIAM KEATING, Massachusetts
DARRELL E. ISSA, California	BRAD SHERMAN, California
PAUL COOK, California	BRIAN HIGGINS, New York
SCOTT PERRY, Pennsylvania	JOAQUIN CASTRO, Texas
REID J. RIBBLE, Wisconsin	ROBIN L. KELLY, Illinois
LEE M. ZELDIN, New York	

CONTENTS

THE U.S.–SAUDI ARABIA COUNTERTERRORISM RELATIONSHIP

TUESDAY, MAY 24, 2016

House of Representatives,
Subcommittee on Terrorism, Nonproliferation, and Trade,
Committee on Foreign Affairs,
Washington, DC.

The subcommittee met, pursuant to notice, at 2 o'clock p.m., in room 2172 Rayburn House Office Building, Hon. Ted Poe (chairman of the subcommittee) presiding.

Mr. Poe. The subcommittee will come to order. The witnesses will take their seats. Without objection, all members may have 5 days to submit statements, questions, and extraneous materials for the record subject to the length limitation in the rules.

Today, the United States and Saudi Arabia work together on maintaining security in the Middle East. Despite the differences between the two countries, we both face the same terrorist enemies that seek our destruction in the post 9/11 era. Our counterterrorism cooperation with Saudi Arabia has increased. According to the Department of Treasury, the kingdom has made improvements in enforcing stringent banking rules that help stem the flow of money to terrorist groups through Saudi financial institutions.

Saudi Arabia is the co-chair of the Counter-ISIL Finance Group, and this group seeks to cut off ISIS from the international finance system. Saudi Arabia has launched aggressive military campaigns in Syria and Yemen, and while the kingdom has taken important steps since 9/11 to counter terrorism, it has some room to improve.

I think we must separate the individuals that live in Saudi Arabia and what they do to support financially terrorism, and the Government of Saudi Arabia. While the Kingdom of Saudi Arabia has adopted strict laws prohibiting terrorist finance, there continue to be press reports about Saudi charities and individual donors funding ISIS, al-Qaeda, and foreign fighters.

The Kingdom of Saudi Arabia still spends billions of dollars every year exporting the Wahhabi interpretation of Islam through its networks of building mosques and schools throughout the world including in the United States. Wahhabism is a fundamentalist form of Islam that insists on a literal interpretation of the Quran. Its 18th century founder Abd al Wahhab in seeking to purify Islam taught that apostates—that is, Christians and Jews and some Muslims—should be persecuted and in some cases killed.

So we should not be surprised that some people practice, when they are taught Wahhabism, violence. While not all followers of

Wahhabism are terrorists, many argue that Wahhabi followers are more easily recruited by terrorist groups.

ISIS openly follows this strict form of Islam and cites Wahhabi clerics, but it does not accept the royal Saudi family as legitimate authorities. Some of the Wahhabi ideology has been exposed in Saudi textbooks and the U.S. has pushed Saudi Arabia to address the problem.

In 2006, the Ambassador at Large for International Religious Freedom John Hanford told Congress the Saudi Government would finish its comprehensive revision of textbooks by 2008. Here we are 8 years later, and the process is still in the future. Where is the new book? As of 2014, high school textbooks worldwide contained offensive materials about Jews, Christians, and others. For example, a 12th grade textbook professes that treachery, betrayal and that annunciation of covenants are among the attributes of the Jews. Another 12th grade textbook asserts that the punishment for conversion away from Islam is execution.

This is somewhat disturbing, and the Saudi Arabian Government needs to be more aggressive in revising these textbooks if that is the goal. The same can be said about sermons given by Saudi clerics as mosques behind closed doors. Researchers have cited hateful messages by clerics that are tantamount to incitement.

Then of course there is the issue that has been brought up again regarding counterterrorism prior to 9/11. 9/11 Commission reports note that Saudi Arabia was long considered a primary source of al-Qaeda funding. There is speculation about the extent of the Saudi Government officials in providing help to 9/11 hijackers, 15 of the 19 hijackers were Saudi nationals.

Then there is the issue of the 28 missing pages in the 9/11 report. I have read the 28 missing pages that the public does not have access to, and I think the public should have access and be able to see those 28 pages. It is my understanding that the Saudi Arabian Government also wants those 28 pages declassified. I think we must make a distinction to some extent between post-9/11 and events that occurred before 9/11.

If a foreign country, any country, can be shown to have significantly supported a terrorist attack on the United States, the victims and their families ought to be able to sue that foreign country no matter who it is. Like any other issue, we should let a jury decide that issue and the damages, if any. As a former judge, I am a great advocate in having litigation in our courts of law to get justice.

If our policy is between American victims and also victims from other parts of the world regarding 9/11 versus our priorities with dealing with foreign countries, I think our Government should always come down on the side of victims and their families of 9/11, without exception.

There are issues dealing with foreign countries, but the 9/11 victims, their families, certainly need justice to occur. Some say that this occurred a long time ago and it is time to move on with our relationships with foreign countries. Fifteen years ago, waiting for justice to occur is too long under our system.

If in fact some other government may have been involved in the 9/11 attacks, I am not saying they were or they weren't, but part of this hearing is to explore this issue as well. The United States national security interest does include working with Saudi Arabia, but the national security interest of the United States also must include making sure that the victims of 9/11 have all of the facts of what occurred on that day that none of us will forget.

I will yield to the ranking member from Massachusetts for his opening statement.

Mr. KEATING. Thank you, Chairman Poe, for conducting this hearing, and I would also like to thank our panel of witnesses who bring with them years of experience and knowledge on the topic of today, Saudi Arabia.

For decades, the United States has maintained strong bilateral relations with the kingdom. Anchored by U.S.-Saudi security cooperation and U.S. concern for global availability of Saudi energy, we have engaged the Saudi Government as a strategic partner to promote regional security and global economic stability.

However, our relationship is deeper than just shared security challenges. It is in both of our countries' interest to strengthen this relationship, yet for us to be mindful that over the last few years shifts in political and economical landscape of the region have shed light on the kingdom's domestic policies. Issues such as political reform, education, human rights, and religious freedom are now more prominent in the U.S.-Saudi relationship than it was in years past.

There is no doubt these sensitive issues have contributed to growing challenges between Washington and Riyadh. In April, President Obama met with Saudi officials. While the visit allayed concerns like making sure our shared security interests remain strong, still, gaps in the fence remain.

Further complicating the relationship is America's increasing energy independence and the recent shale oil boom that has produced our imports, increased imports and increased our exports when it comes to oil. Saudi Arabia and other OPEC members rely on American markets to refine their systems and bring to the market heavy sour crude oil.

As we continue to witness the evolution of this region through the lens of the administration's final year, it is important that we consider our own objectives. It is the responsibility of the United States to keep our foreign policy objectives close in mind as we assess our bilateral relations with partners and whether they promote or hinder these goals.

Of particular concern to me is the credibility of our shared counterterrorism operations and intentions. While our two countries have worked successfully to address counterterrorism threats and the financing of those threats through intelligence sharing and monitoring compliance, other actions may complicate these efforts. For example, Riyadh's campaign in Yemen has changed our efforts to combat al-Qaeda in the Arabian Peninsula, and domestic counterterrorism efforts have directly targeted human rights activists and peaceful protestors who have been tried in Saudi in terrorism tribunals.

I look forward to hearing from our witnesses in regarding the future of the United States and Saudi in terms of their relationships and how we can work together to align mutual goals and promote a more open society. I yield back, Mr. Chairman.

4

Mr. POE. I thank the ranking member. The chair will now recognize other members for a 1-minute opening statement. The chair recognizes Mr. Issa from California for 1 minute.

Mr. ISSA. Thank you, Mr. Chairman, and thank you for holding this important hearing today. There are two committees that will be looking at the proposal that has come from the Senate, this committee and Judiciary. The Judiciary Committee has to look, quite frankly, at U.S. law and whether litigation against the sovereign nation is appropriate. We as a committee have to look at the world. We have to look at the bigger question. What if we do this without an affirmative, specific foreknowledge of wrongdoing by a representative at a high level of the Saudi Government?

The answer is clear. If we look at it and allow discovery, a poking around, a typical plaintiff's trial lawyer look-see, then in fact the rest of the world will likely respond. If the rest of the world likely responds, there is no question but that actions of U.S. persons or U.S. entities, including but not limited to our intelligence community, will have us in courts around the world.

It is our responsibility both here at this committee and when looking at highly classified documents to reach a conclusion of whether or not this case should be allowed to go forward before allowing discovery outside of the U.S. Government. I thank the chairman for his yielding, and yield back.

Mr. POE. I thank the gentleman from California. The chair recognizes another gentleman from California, Mr. Sherman, for an opening statement.

Mr. SHERMAN. Our laws already provide an exception to sovereign immunity for those who are state sponsors of terrorism. It seems only a slight increase in that to say it should apply if the plaintiffs are able to show that the foreign government engaged in terrorism here in the United States.

But as important as it is to have our judicial system work for the benefit of victims, it may be that it is up to the United States to compensate the victims as we have to some degree. And the most important thing is not punishing those who committed or supported this act, but preventing the next act of terrorism.

What concerns me is the Saudi Government comes to us and says they are our friend and we should protect them from this statute, while funding every day the Wahhabi mullahs who not only preach orthodox practice of Islam but preach violent murder against those who they disagree with. And it is time for Saudi Arabia to come clean. They can't say they don't support terrorism. All they do is fund at the hundreds of millions of dollars a year those who plant the seeds of terrorism around the world. I yield back.

Mr. POE. I thank the gentleman. The chair recognizes the gentleman from South Carolina, Mr. Wilson.

Mr. WILSON. Thank you, Mr. Chairman, for holding this important hearing on the critical relationship between the United States and Saudi Arabia.

For over 70 years, both countries have had a close economic partnership beginning with the establishment of the Arab American Oil Company, Aramco, by the Standard Oil Company in 1944.

In recent decades, Saudi Arabia has made substantial progress in their counterterrorism efforts post 9/11. They have strengthened financial policies aimed at countering terrorist financing and worked with the United States and other countries to increase transparency and information sharing. They have also imposed harsh sentences on Saudi nationals who attempt to join foreign terror groups and have conducted military operations against the Islamic State and other terrorist organizations in the region. These are all important steps in working toward peace and security for the region.

As we work together to combat Islamic extremism, we must keep in mind the considerable influence that Saudi Arabia has over the ideologies and religious practices that will guide the Middle East for years to come. I look forward to hearing from our witnesses on the future of U.S.-Saudi Arabia terrorism relationship. Again, I appreciate the leadership of our chairman, Chairman Judge Ted Poe, and I yield back.

Mr. POE. I thank the gentleman. The chair recognizes the gentleman from California, Mr. Rohrabacher, for 1 minute.

Mr. ROHRABACHER. Thank you very much, Mr. Chairman, for holding this hearing. It is long overdue. How many Americans have to die? How many of our innocent citizens are blown up or are murdered from a terrorist act that we are ignoring, intentionally ignoring who is financing those acts.

I think it is clear to all of us who have been active in Washington over the years that the Saudis and the Saudi royal family have been right up to their eyeballs in terrorist activity and supporting the terrorist activity of radical Islamic forces in the Middle East. It is up to us to call the truth, to say the truth. We are not going to correct the situation. It won't get better unless we are willing to step up and basically let the American people know who is the bad guy and who is the good guy in this age of terrorism.

Mr. POE. I thank the gentleman. Without objection, all members may have 5 days to submit statements, questions, extraneous materials for the record subject to the length limitation in the rules. And without objection, all witnesses' prepared statements will be made part of the record.

I ask that each witness keep your presentation to no more than 5 minutes. I will introduce each witness. I do want to thank all four of you for being here early, on time before we ever started, supposed to start this hearing, but as you all know votes got in the way. So I do appreciate your patience.

Ambassador Tim Roemer is a former Member of Congress and a former U.S. Ambassador to India. While he was in Congress he sat on the House Intelligence Committee and was a member of the 9/11 Commission.

Mr. Simon Henderson is the Baker Fellow and director of the Gulf and Energy Policy Program at Washington Institute for Near East Policy. He has written two studies of the Saudi royal family, both of which were published by The Washington Institute.

And Mrs. Karen Elliot House is currently a senior fellow at the Belfer Center for Science and International Affairs at Harvard's Kennedy School of Government. She is the author of the book on Saudi Arabia: Its People, Past, Religion, Fault Lines—and Future.

6

And Dr. Daniel Byman is a professor at Georgetown University's School of Foreign Service. He has served on the 9/11 Commission staff and has testified numerous times before this committee.

Ambassador Roemer, we will start with you. You have 5 minutes.

STATEMENT OF THE HONORABLE TIM ROEMER, PH.D. (FORMER 9/11 COMMISSIONER)

Mr. ROEMER. Thank you very much. Mr. Chairman, Mr. Ranking Member Keating, fellow members, I ask unanimous consent the entirety of my statement be entered into the record, and I would recognize a special guest I have here today, my son Matthew Roemer who just graduated from Wake Forest University.

Mr. POE. Without objection——

Mr. ROEMER. Thank you, Mr. Chairman.

Mr. POE [continuing]. Your comments will be made part of the record. And we do recognize your son who is a recent graduate of Wake Forest.

Mr. ROEMER. Thank you, sir.

Throughout the history of our engagement with the kingdom our relationship with Saudi Arabia has been strategically crucial yet a challenging one and at times a very demanding one. Saudi Arabia sits at the crossroads of so many critical issues for American foreign policy interests—terrorism, Iran, Middle East stability, energy, and human rights.

Serving on the 9/11 Commission, we noted that the U.S.-Saudi relationship had been in the dark for too long. Both countries' governments recognized the value in working closely together, but neither was willing to make the case for the relationship in public to argue for its merits and its shortcomings.

The 9/11 Commission recommended over 10 years ago, "The problems in the U.S.-Saudi relationship must be confronted openly. It should include a shared interest in greater tolerance and cultural respect translating into a commitment to fight the violent extremists who foment hatred." Ten years ago we said that.

Today we still struggle to talk directly about our relationship with the kingdom. In light of this fact, I would like to thank this committee for holding this hearing on this subject bringing greater transparency and clarity to American diplomacy and to the American people.

The Saudis pose a number of challenges for the United States and its foreign policy. Saudi society still continues to produce a disturbing number of recruits and supporters for terrorist groups around the world including in Syria. Moreover, according to a front page article in the New York Times just this past Sunday titled, "How Kosovo Was Turned into a Fertile Ground for ISIS," Saudi influence and money has transformed this once tolerant Muslim society into a "font of Islamic extremism and pipeline for jihadists."

Domestically, the Saudi Government still continues to have a poor record on human rights. The Saudis are fighting a war in Yemen with goals different than the United States, thus creating some problems for the United States in the Middle East. These are signs, ladies and gentlemen, that the United States and Saudi Arabia still have much work to do in this crucial partnership; and it is a partnership.

I believe that our relationship with the kingdom is crucial to our interests in the Middle East. Addressing our concerns diplomatically and privately is often the appropriate path. As a former diplomat we often did this behind closed doors, however, sometimes we must honestly and openly confront our legitimate differences. Friends and allies cannot bury their disagreements. They must frankly address them and counterterrorism must be at the top of the American and the Saudi list.

Counterterrorism. After 9/11, the news that 15 of the 19 hijackers had come from Saudi Arabia led many Americans to question whether the Saudis were the ally we thought them to be. They continue to be our ally, but an embattled one. Furthermore, we found that Saudi Arabia was fertile ground for fundraising and support for al-Qaeda. In the 9/11 Commission report we did not discover high level and direct Saudi Government involvement in the plot, but wrote that Saudi Arabia had been a problematic ally in the fight against terrorism.

There is a glaring contrast some days and weeks and months between high level Saudi legitimate cooperation in helping the United States uncover plots, which is critical for us, but it often directly conflicts with the society and culture that sometimes exports extremism and intolerance.

There has been recent media attention to these 28 pages that Judge Poe just cited, classified information actually written by Congress in the Joint Intelligence Committee, but was reviewed and investigated by the 9/11 Commission. I served on both of these panels. I am strongly in favor for declassifying this information as quickly and as soon as possible. For national security reasons the 9/11 families deserve it, the American people deserve it, and justice deserves it.

We have the right as Americans to transparency and sunlight, not the darkness that conspiracy theories thrive on in today's cynical political climate. While the 28 pages are important to declassify—we need to get those out—it is crucial to understand the unclassified 9/11 Commission report, particularly Chapters 5, 7, and the footnotes where we talk about some of the problems that are ongoing today in Saudi society to export extremism, fund radical ideology for terrorist groups, and supply a stream of jihadists around the world.

We have seen, no doubt, improvements from the kingdom. It has created a deradicalization program and is helping to reintegrate extremists back into society in a regular fashion. Saudi intelligence agencies have worked very closely with their American counterparts to share information about threats from extremist groups, most notably a tip-off in 2010 which reportedly led to the disruption of a plot to bomb U.S. cargo planes.

They also briefly participated in the U.S. war, led against the Islamic State, coalition in Syria. According to the most recent State Department Country Reports on Terrorism, the Saudis have instituted a number of legal reforms to strengthen the prohibitions on supporting terrorism.

These are crucial tools in fighting terrorism, but sometimes they are not sufficient strategic ones. Saudi Arabia has outlawed terrorist groups like the Islamic State and banned its citizens from providing financial support to them. Yet despite these official acts, studies on the background of Islamic State foreign fighters continue to show that Saudi recruits are among the most numerous among the group's ranks.

A recent West Point study confirmed that Saudi recruits were in the highest three groups in Syria. The threat of extremism cannot be countered by police, intelligence and military actions alone. The Saudi Government needs to address the threat of radicalization and extremism within its own society.

In all of this we should be cognizant of the fact that the Saudis themselves are threatened by extremism and have suffered greatly from it. In 2003, Saudi al-Qaeda terrorists unleashed a campaign of attacks in that country that shocked the kingdom. The Saudis took immediate steps to address this.

I want to speak for a moment, Mr. Chairman, about Iran. Iran's support for terrorism is a serious threat to Middle East stability, American interests, and American allies in the region. In the face of these threats we must make sure that Saudi Arabia, the focus of so much of Iran's attention and ambitions, is able to resist and appropriately confront Tehran's attempts to influence the region.

How we manage this makes vital difference to our friends and allies in the Middle East. We cannot allow Saudi Arabia's justified fears of its neighbor to lead to deeper disagreements within and with the United States. While we work together to counter some of Iran's nefarious efforts to stoke instability in the region, this must not distract from the fight against terrorist threats like al-Qaeda and the Islamic State.

Mr. Chairman, I will skip through some comments on energy. I want to conclude on a human rights topic. Congress helped create the United States Commission on International Religious Freedom in 1998 in order to promote the fundamental human rights of people to worship and observe their faith in peace.

Since its creation, the Commission, at the urging I might add of Congress, has done valuable work uncovering examples of intolerance, anti-Semitism, and incitement to violence in Saudi textbooks provided to schools in developing countries all over the world. The Islamic State has even discovered and utilized this material in some of their textbooks to reflect their world view. One scholar has even noted the use of this material in schools under the Islamic State's control in Raqqa, Syria.

While the kingdom has made some progress in revising its textbooks and curtailing extremist material, and we note that and encourage that, this Commission notes that the Saudi Government still includes highly offensive references in their high school textbooks.

So to conclude, members of this important subcommittee, having served in both the legislative and the executive branches of American Government, I have seen the important role that congressional oversight and your counsel plays in shaping American foreign policy.

The U.S.-Saudi relationship is an area where Congress must continue to play an important role with the executive branch and for the American people. Congress should continue to hold oversight hearings, insist on better progress on counterterrorism results from Saudi Arabia, and discuss the human rights situation.

The U.S. Intelligence Community gives credits to Saudi Arabia for developing and cooperating on counterintelligence and helping stop specific attacks. We are grateful for this. While this is true, we must see more consistent results from Saudi Arabia on preventing the export of intolerance and extremism around the world; we must work together to curtail the financial support for al-Qaeda and terrorist groups; we must see more results on reducing the Saudi supply of the high number of foreign fighters in Syria.

Resetting and rebuilding this decades-long strategic partnership with Saudi will be a foreign policy priority for the United States in 2017. And I thank the chairman and ranking member and members for my testimony.

[The prepared statement of Mr. Roemer follows:]

UNCLASSIFIED

**Written Testimony of
Tim Roemer**

**To the House Foreign Affairs Subcommittee on Terrorism,
Nonproliferation & Trade
Under the House Committee on Foreign Affairs
Hearing: "The U.S.-Saudi Arabia Counterterrorism Relationship"**

May 24, 2016

Chairman Poe, Ranking Member Keating, and Members of the Subcommittee: thank you for this opportunity to address the Subcommittee on the U.S-Saudi Counterterrorism Relationship.

Throughout the history of our engagement with the Kingdom, our relationship with Saudi Arabia has been strategically crucial, yet a challenging one and at times a very demanding one. Saudi Arabia sits at the crossroads of so many critical issues for American foreign policy interests: terrorism, Iran, Middle East stability, Energy and human rights.

Serving on the 9/11 Commission, we noted that the U.S.-Saudi relationship had been in the dark for too long. Both countries' governments recognized the value in working closely together but neither was willing to make the case for the relationship in public, to argue its merits and identify its shortcomings. The 9/11 Commission recommended over 10 years ago, "The problems in the US- Saudi relationship must be confronted, openly. ... It should include a shared interest in greater tolerance and cultural respect, translating into a commitment to fight the violent extremists who foment hatred."

Today, we still struggle to talk directly about our relationship with the Kingdom. In light of this fact, I would like to thank this committee for holding a hearing on this subject and bringing greater transparency and clarity to American diplomacy.

The Saudis pose a number of challenges for the United States and its foreign policy. Saudi society still continues to produce a disturbing number of recruits and supporters for terrorist groups around the world. Domestically, the Saudi government still continues to have a poor record on human rights. The Saudis are fighting a war in Yemen with different goals than the United States.

These are signs that the United States and Saudi Arabia still have much work to do. I believe that our relationship with the Kingdom is crucial to our interests in the Middle East. Addressing our concerns diplomatically and privately is often the appropriate path. However, sometimes we must honestly and openly confront our differences. Friends and allies cannot bury their disagreements; they must honestly address them.

Counterterrorism

After 9/11, the news that 15 of the 19 hijackers involved in the attack had come from Saudi Arabia led many Americans to question whether the Saudis were the ally we thought them to be. Furthermore we found that Saudi Arabia was fertile ground for fundraising and support for Al Qaeda. In the 9/11 Commission Report, we did not discover high-level and direct Saudi government involvement in the plot. We wrote that Saudi Arabia had been a "problematic ally" in the fight against terrorism. There is a contrast between high-level official Saudi cooperation against terrorist plots directly conflicting with a society and culture exporting extremism and intolerance.

Since then, we have seen some improvements from the Kingdom on a number of fronts. It has created a de-radicalization program aimed at helping to reintegrate extremists back into society. Saudi intelligence agencies have also worked closely with their American counterparts to share information about threats from extremist groups — most notably providing a tipoff in 2010 which reportedly led to the disruption of a plot to bomb U.S.-bound cargo planes. They have also briefly participated in the air war over Syria led by the U.S.-supported anti-Islamic State coalition. According to the most recent State Department Country Reports on Terrorism, the Saudis have instituted a number of legal reforms to strengthen the prohibitions on supporting terrorism.

These are crucial tools in fighting terrorism, but they are not sufficiently strategic ones. Saudi Arabia has outlawed terrorist groups like the Islamic State and banned its citizens from providing financial support to them. Yet despite these official acts, studies on the backgrounds of Islamic State foreign fighters continue to show that Saudi recruits are among the most numerous within the group's ranks.

The threat of extremism cannot be countered by police, intelligence, and military actions alone. The Saudi government needs to address the threat of radicalization and extremism within its own society. It needs to stop supporting religious leaders who promote messages of hate, intolerance, and violence against different religions. Deeper structural reforms are also needed.

In all of this, we should be cognizant that the Saudis themselves are threatened by extremism and have suffered greatly from it. In 2003, Saudi al-Qaeda terrorists unleashed a campaign of attacks in the country which shocked the Kingdom. The Saudis took resolute and immediate steps to address this. In the years following those attacks, Saudi and Yemeni terrorists have spawned a formidable and deadly regional affiliate, al-Qaeda in the Arabian Peninsula. This is a lethal and menacing threat to the United States.

Iran

Iran's support for terrorism is a serious threat to Middle East stability, American interests and American allies in the Middle East. It not only promotes terrorism, but also tries to subvert and destabilize governments in the region and continues to work on a ballistic missile program that threatens the Gulf States, Israel and our European allies.

In the face of these threats, we must make sure that Saudi Arabia, the focus of so much of Iran's attention and ambitions, is able to strongly resist and appropriately confront Tehran's attempts to dominate the region. How we manage this makes a vital difference to our friends and allies in the Middle East. We cannot allow Saudi Arabia's justified fears of its neighbor to lead it to deeper disagreements with the United States. While we work together to counter Iran's nefarious efforts to stoke instability in the region, this must not distract from the fight against terrorist threats like al-Qaeda and the Islamic State.

The Joint Comprehensive Plan of Action which placed a number of restrictions on Iran's nuclear program was an important step in potentially containing the threat from Tehran but it cannot be the final one. The Saudis look across the Gulf and see a growing ballistic missile program pointed at them. They look north to Iraq and see Iranian-backed militias and terrorist groups weakening the Iraqi state and carrying out sectarian attacks against Sunni civilians under the guise of fighting the Islamic State. They look to Syria and see Iranian-backed militias, Hezbollah terrorists and Iranian Revolutionary Guard Corps officers supporting the Assad regime in its brutal war against Syrian civilians.

In the face of these threats, the Saudis and other Gulf states are understandably nervous and anxious. It is the responsibility of American foreign policy to provide steady reassurance that the United States has the current capability and direct will to provide security in the region, particularly in the event of a crisis.

We also need to make sure that the U.S.-Saudi relationship can address both the threat from Iran and the threat of terrorist groups like al-Qaeda and the Islamic State simultaneously, without detracting from each other. Saudi Arabia made an initially important contribution to the military campaign against the Islamic State in Syria but it has since grown distracted by a lengthy and seemingly stalled war against Iranian-backed proxies in Yemen. The chaos, civilian casualties, and the collateral damage to schools and hospitals, have been catastrophic.

Energy

As we know, the downturn in the price of oil will pose challenges for Saudi Arabia both economically and politically. These changes hold both promise and peril for the Kingdom. Change is difficult and sometimes painful. But the pressures that Saudi Arabia now faces could also be an opportunity for them to modernize Saudi society, reform their government and further promote moderation and tolerance.

The price of oil has dipped and peaked before and the Saudis have weathered these ups and downs without severe consequences for their political stability. In the short term, there is little cause to believe this will change dramatically.

However, the availability of new sources of oil production in the United States adds greater competition in energy markets and may constrain the ability of oil producers to bring oil prices back up to their previous heights over the longer term.

Consequently, the constraints on oil markets mean Saudi Arabia will have to prepare its people, economy and government for a world where oil revenue can no longer completely insulate them from the global marketplace. The Saudis have realized they need to diversify their economy to include new sectors aside from energy. To accomplish that, the Saudis will have to reform their educational institutions to focus more on broader skill development. They will need to address the current model of attracting hundreds of foreign workers to low-wage jobs.

In the face of greater competition in energy markets and lower prices over the long term creating significant budget issues, the Saudi government has launched a new initiative called Saudi Vision 2030. This might lead to renegotiating the social contract that has governed the country for so long. Saudi citizens may demand more of a say in their own governance, in their education system, and in their economic opportunities.

Human Rights

The section on Saudi Arabia in the Country Reports on Human Rights Practices for 2015 put out by the State Department's Bureau of Democracy, Human Rights and Labor, stated the following: "The most important human rights problems reported included citizens' lack of the ability and legal means to choose their government; restriction on universal rights, such as freedom of expression, including on the Internet, and the freedom of assembly, association, movement, and religion; and pervasive gender discrimination and lack of equal rights that affected all aspects of women's lives." This makes a rather grim and challenging environment for Saudi Arabia.

Congress helped create the United States Commission on International Religious Freedom in 1998 in order to promote the fundamental human right of people to worship and observe their faith in peace. Since its creation, the Commission, at the urging of Congress, has done valuable work uncovering examples of intolerance, anti-Semitism and incitement to violence in Saudi textbooks provided to schools in developing countries around the world. The Islamic State has discovered and utilized the material in some of these textbooks to reflect its world view. One scholar has noted the use of this material in schools under the Islamic State's control in Raqqa, Syria.[1] While the Kingdom has made some progress in revising its textbooks and curtailing extremist material, this Commission notes that the Saudi government still includes highly offensive references in their high school text books.[2]

Conclusion

Having served in both the legislative and executive branches of American government, I have seen the important role that Congressional oversight and counsel play in shaping American foreign policy for the better. The U.S.-Saudi relationship is an area where Congress must continue to play a role with the executive branch and for the American people.

The U.S. Intelligence Community gives credit to Saudi Arabia for cooperating on counter-intelligence and helping stop specific attacks. While this is true, we must see more consistent results on preventing the export of intolerance and extremism around the world; we must work together to further prevent financial support for al Qaeda and terrorists groups; and we must work towards reducing the Saudi supply of high numbers of foreign fighters In Syria. Resetting and rebuilding this decades-long partnership and strategic relationship will be a foreign policy priority in 2017.

---

[1] William McCants, "The ISIS Apocalypse: The History, Strategy, and Doomsday Vision of the Islamic State," St. Martin's Press, September 22, 2015

[2] U.S. Commission on International Religious Freedom, Annual Report, 2016 and 2014 Report on International Religious Freedom, State Department, October 14, 2015.
http://www.state.gov/j/drl/rls/irf/2014/nea/238476.htm

Mr. POE. Thank you, Ambassador.
Mr. Henderson.

STATEMENT OF MR. SIMON HENDERSON, DIRECTOR, GULF AND ENERGY POLICY PROGRAM, THE WASHINGTON INSTITUTE FOR NEAR EAST POLICY

Mr. HENDERSON. Thank you. Chairman Poe, Ranking Member Keating, distinguished members of the committee; it is an honor and privilege to appear before you today. I have written about Saudi Arabia, particularly the royal family known as the House of Saud, for more than 20 years. Arguably, I publish more about Saudi Arabia, ten analyses so far this year, than anyone else. I also have a reputation for detailed reporting which probably explains why I have never been to Saudi Arabia. I have never been given a visa to visit there although I have traveled widely in the rest of the Middle East.

Saudi Arabia sees itself as the leader of the Islamic world, a leader if not the leader of the Arab world, and by virtue of it being the world's largest oil exporter, a leader of the energy world. Of these leadership roles, it is the Islamic one which is from a Saudi perspective by far the most important. Within the kingdom are Islam's two holiest places, Mecca and Medina. Ensuring the safety of Muslim pilgrims who thereby recognize Saudi leadership is a paramount concern.

This emphasis on Islam was a feature of a memorable memo written by a departing British Ambassador 32 years ago. He identified three principal features of the kingdom. Islam was one of them, insularity was another—it is a very closed society, or was at that point—and he also noted that the kingdom was incompetent, a feature which I often ask friends who have visited the kingdom whether it is still valid or not and they suggest that it is. And that is a word which perhaps partly explains our concern about Saudi counterterrorism efforts.

Apart from Islam, a major influence on Saudi thinking is history, particularly recent history. I would argue that the two most important events in Saudi minds both date back to 1979. In February of that year, the Islamic Revolution in Iran overthrew the Shah and brought to power a clerical regime of Shiite Muslims, the majority faith in Iran. As Shiites, they are historical rivals of Sunni Muslims such as Saudis. The ethnic difference of Iranians mostly being Persians rather than Arabs is also significant.

Later the same year, in November 1979, the Grand Mosque in Mecca was seized by Sunni militants, contesting the legitimacy of the House of Saud. It was 2 weeks before Saudi soldiers, with the embarrassingly necessary assistance of French special forces, regained control. Since then, the House of Saud has had to fight on two contradictory fronts: Countering regional Iranian mischief including support for the kingdom's own minority Shiite community, while also dealing with Sunni extremists including potential jihadists, at home.

The principal challenge for the U.S.-Saudi counterterrorism relationship is that right now there is more than the usual amount of differences on emphasis and direction which can apply to even close allies. It has to be significant that in the recent profile of

President Obama in The Atlantic, Saudi Arabia was criticized more severely and more often than any other country, ally or not.

A new and challenging dimension in the relationship was introduced a year ago when King Abdullah died and was replaced by King Salman. Three months after that the line of succession changed. The Crown Prince was sacked and he was replaced by the Deputy Crown Prince Muhammad bin Nayef, and more significantly, the number three slot of the Deputy Crown Prince was taken by King Salman's younger son Muhammad bin Salman who is just 30 years old.

At the moment, we are facing an uncertain future. Washington's principal partner on counterterrorism issues for the last decade or so, Muhammad bin Nayef, has been marginalized but the need for an effective counterterrorism partnership is as great as ever. Also, Riyadh is distrustful of Washington's approach to what the Saudi sees as at least half of the terrorism problem, Iran.

In these circumstances, the United States cannot take for granted its current counterterrorism partnership with Saudi Arabia. Despite differences and public insults, the relationship needs to adapt so the substance of it can be sustained during the continuing period of political uncertainty and especially within the House of Saud and where the real power lies. Thank you.

[The prepared statement of Mr. Henderson follows:]

Bilateral Counterterrorism Cooperation and Changes in Saudi Leadership

Simon Henderson

Baker Fellow and Director, Gulf and Energy Policy Program,
The Washington Institute for Near East Policy

Testimony submitted to the U.S. House Committee on Foreign Affairs, Subcommittee on Terrorism, Nonproliferation, and Trade

May 24, 2016

Chairman Royce, Ranking Member Engel, distinguished members of the committee, it is an honor and privilege to appear before you today. I have written about Saudi Arabia, particularly the royal family known as the House of Saud, for more than twenty years. Arguably, I publish more about Saudi Arabia -- ten analyses so far this year -- than anyone else. I also have a reputation for detailed reporting, which probably explains why I have never been given a visa to visit Saudi Arabia, though I have traveled widely in the rest of the Middle East.

I would like to offer you several ways, templates if you like, with which to view the kingdom:

Firstly, Saudi Arabia sees itself as the leader of the Islamic world; a leader, if not the leader, of the Arab world; and, by virtue of it being the world's largest oil exporter, a leader of the energy world. Of these leadership roles, it is the Islamic one which is, from a Saudi perspective, by far the most important. Within the kingdom are Islam's two holiest places, Mecca and Medina. Ensuring the safety of Muslim pilgrims -- who thereby recognize Saudi leadership -- is a paramount concern.

Secondly, within the kingdom, the three main components of power are the House of Saud, the Islamic clerical establishment (known as the ulama), and the commercial/technocratic elite. The latter two -- the ulama and the business community -- are rivals. The royal family has to balance concessions to one with concessions to the other. Figuratively, it is like a triangle. Each group has its own corner but the triangle is in constant tension, twisting backwards and forwards as one group or another seeks advantage.

Thirdly, in 1984, a departing British ambassador memorably encapsulated his tour of duty by identifying the principal features of the kingdom as being "incompetence, insularity, and Islam."[1] The ambassador liked the Saudis but found them "feckless, disorganized, and unconscientious." Additionally, he noted that Saudis consider themselves as different from other Arabs, a view reciprocated by non-Saudi Arabs. Referring to non-Arabs in the kingdom, the ambassador wrote: "They really cannot be bothered with foreigners." Instead the Saudis look inward to their family and extended family, which also makes them tend to be conservative. The ambassador concluded that Islam is the central feature of the kingdom and is also a source of social strength.

---

[1] British Foreign and Commonwealth Office, Diplomatic Report No. 51/84, "Valedictory Number Two: The Saudi Arabians," Jeddah, Saudi Arabia, June 24, 1984.

Much has happened in the thirty-plus years since the ambassador wrote those words. I regularly inquire of friends who go to the kingdom whether his fundamental judgment is now wrong. My understanding is that the essence of his remarks remains valid.

Apart from Islam, a further major influence on Saudi thinking is history, particularly recent history. The two most important events in Saudi minds date back to 1979.

In February of that year the Islamic Revolution in Iran overthrew the Shah and brought to power a clerical regime of Shiite Muslims, the majority faith in Iran. As Shiites, they are historical rivals of Sunni Muslims such as Saudis. Their victory empowered Shiite minorities across the Middle East, in Lebanon, Iraq, Bahrain, and also Saudi Arabia, places where traditionally Shiites had effectively been second-class citizens. The ethnic difference of Iranians mostly being Persians rather than Arabs is also significant.

Later the same year, in November 1979, the Grand Mosque in Mecca was seized by Sunni militants, contesting the legitimacy of the House of Saud. It was two weeks before Saudi soldiers, with the embarrassingly necessary assistance of French special forces, regained control.

Since then, the House of Saud has had to fight on two contradictory fronts: countering regional Iranian mischief, including support for the kingdom's own minority Shiite community, while also dealing with Sunni extremists -- including potential jihadists -- at home.

Further events are at least a partial consequence of Saudi action or inaction: the attack on a U.S. military housing compound in al-Khobar in 1996 (by Shiite militants); the terror attacks of 9/11 (conducted by Sunni militants); the attacks on housing compounds for foreigners in Riyadh in 2003 (again by Sunni militants); and the chaos of the "Arab Spring," where Riyadh wanted regime changes in Syria and Yemen but was upset when President Mubarak of Egypt was overthrown. The kingdom also remains almost paranoid about Iran, deeply fearful about the regional consequences of the 2015 Iran nuclear accord, and disappointed by President Obama's style of leadership.

These Saudi attitudes are of immense consequence for U.S. policy. Saudi Arabia and the United States have been allies for decades, and the U.S. is the kingdom's most valued non-Arab ally, particularly in deterring external threats against the House of Saud. Washington's motivations are various but they come down to the need for stability in an area that is the center of the energy world and also the Islamic world -- two issues which have dominated news headlines for decades because of disruption and strife. The region's very instability also endangers other U.S. allies and interests. And the U.S. homeland continues to be a potential target of terrorists and plots emanating from the Middle East.

The principal challenge for the U.S.-Saudi counterterrorism relationship is that there is more than the usual amount of differences on emphasis and direction, which can apply to even close allies. On Yemen, Washington thinks the Saudi-led military action, now more than a year old, was misconceived and is going nowhere. Additionally, Iran's role in supporting the Houthi rebels has been exaggerated by Riyadh. Furthermore, the U.S. view is that, instead of heading in the direction of calming the tension between Tehran and Riyadh, there is a danger of escalation. It has to be significant that in the recent profile of President Obama in the *Atlantic*, Saudi Arabia was criticized more severely and more often than any other country, ally or not.[2]

One major issue for the U.S., along with other countries, is that in Saudi perceptions of domestic security, threats are so broadly defined -- effectively from terrorism to texting. Advocates of what would be regarded elsewhere as freedom of speech are dealt with in the same manner and the same special courts as those using violence against the government. Punishment can be draconian and almost random. International opinion was profoundly

---

[2] Jeffrey Goldberg, "The Obama Doctrine," *Atlantic*, April 2016.

disturbed by the execution on January 2 this year of no less than forty-seven men accused of various terrorist offenses, some of whom had been on death row for many years. The vast majority were Sunnis with links to al-Qaeda or the Islamic State, but four of those executed were Shiites, including a firebrand preacher by the name of Nimr al-Nimr. In an apparent gesture of fairness, the ratio of forty-three to four is roughly the estimated proportion of Sunnis to Shiites living in Saudi Arabia.

The timing of the executions was seen as sending a message to Shiite extremists supported by Iran, as well as Sunni jihadists, that the kingdom was going to be tough on terrorism. But Riyadh probably did not expect the strength of the reaction. An Iranian mob, almost certainly encouraged by the authorities, sacked and burned the Saudi embassy in Tehran. Riyadh promptly broke off diplomatic relations with Iran, encouraging its Arab allies to do likewise, though most only withdrew their ambassadors -- a lack of unity surely noticed by Iran.

In recent years, the public description of the state of U.S.-Saudi counterterrorism cooperation has been platitudinous, as if any hint of open criticism is counterproductive. But a new and challenging dimension has been introduced in Saudi Arabia since the change of leadership brought about in January 2015, when King Abdullah died. He had been the effective leader for twenty years, though the actual monarch only from 2005. Abdullah was succeeded by his half-brother, Salman, who initially named another half-brother, Muqrin, as his crown prince, and a nephew, Muhammad bin Nayef (MbN), as deputy crown prince. MbN has been a Washington favorite, dubbed "Mr. Counterterrorism" and admired for surviving, at least physically almost unscathed, a suicide bomb attack in 2009.

But in April 2015, three months after Salman's accession, the line of succession changed. Muqrin was sacked. Although he was replaced as heir apparent by MbN, more significantly the number three slot was taken by one of King Salman's younger sons, Muhammad bin Salman (MbS), who is just thirty years old.

At eighty this year, King Salman remains very visible, though reportedly with a range of health issues. There is now little doubt that the monarch wants his son, MbS, to be the next king rather than MbN. How that happens, when it happens, and the consequences of it happening are a matter of conjecture. In the meantime, MbS is in charge of economic policy, including oil policy, and he is the minister of defense running the war in Yemen. MbN, who is reportedly fifty-six years old, is still the minister of interior and chairs the weekly cabinet meetings when the king is absent, but his power and influence appear to be waning. His much younger cousin MbS is the person of consequence for all major issues in Riyadh. MbN, Washington's man, has been sidelined.

At this time, tried and tested ways of understanding the power politics of the Saudi royal family need to be discarded. The House of Saud has traditionally valued age (meaning seniority) and experience for its leadership positions. Disagreement and rivalry has been countered by the perceived need for consensus and a common public front to be displayed to the nation as well as the world. At just thirty years old, Muhammad bin Salman lacks age as well as experience. Furthermore, since his father became crown prince in 2012 and MbS became the head of his court, there have been a profusion of tales about MbS's high-handed tactics with royal cousins, so it is doubtful whether his further promotion has much support within the wider royal family.

So we are facing an uncertain future. Washington's principal partner on counterterrorism issues for the last decade or so, Muhammad bin Nayef, has been marginalized, but the need for an effective counterterrorism partnership is as great as ever. Also, Riyadh is distrustful of Washington's approach to what the Saudi side sees as at least half of its terrorism problem -- Iran.

In these circumstances, the United States cannot take for granted its current counterterrorism partnership with Saudi Arabia. Despite differences and public insults, the relationship needs to adapt so that the substance of it can be sustained during the continuing period of political uncertainty about real power in the House of Saud.

Mr. POE. Thank you, Mr. Henderson.

Ms. House. Microphone.

STATEMENT OF MS. KAREN ELLIOT HOUSE, SENIOR FELLOW, BELFER CENTER FOR SCIENCE AND INTERNATIONAL AFFAIRS

Ms. HOUSE. Oh, excuse me, I am saying in my best Texas accent, Mr. Chairman and Ranking Member Mr. Keating.

Mr. POE. And I can understand you a whole lot better than I can Mr. Henderson, that is for sure.

Ms. HOUSE. Yes, I knew you wouldn't need a translator for me. The others may.

I am going to focus on Saudi Arabia itself because much is changing in the kingdom these days. A new generation of young Saudi leaders is now in charge after nearly six decades of rule by aged and increasingly infirm sons of the founder. Also changing, unfortunately, is the U.S.-Saudi relationship which was built on the tacit understanding of Saudi oil for U.S. support and protection.

On my latest visit there in January, the most recent of dozens of visits over the last 38 years—I began going as a reporter for the Wall Street Journal—I found Saudi royals and a lot of Saudi citizens, the number one question they wanted to ask is, is the U.S. policy of avoiding involvement in Middle East problems permanent or will a new administration, a new U.S. President again exert traditional leadership in the Middle East including support for our Saudi ally?

Obviously, with the Presidential election some months away we don't know what the next administration's policy would be, but the point I want to make is I believe it is clear already that the future of Saudi Arabia with this new generation of leaders for some of the reasons Simon mentioned, with this new generation of leaders in charge is of critical importance to us.

Despite the fact that the U.S. produces more oil than any time in 30 years, we are still dependent on the global oil market even though only 8 percent of our oil comes from Saudi Arabia. And secondly, obviously as been mentioned by the chairman and others, Saudi Arabia is the wellspring of this religious Wahhabi philosophy that motivates at least some of the jihadi hatred that seeks to destroy the Western way of life. So for those reasons, I think it is critically important that U.S. policymakers understand the forces at work in the kingdom.

Support for Saudi stability and Israeli democracy have been two of the key U.S. goals in the Middle East, certainly in my whole lifetime, and in my view they must remain so. The new generation of leadership in Riyadh has a vision—I stress the word vision—to transform the Saudi economy and to some extent its society that will benefit, in my view, not only Saudi citizens but also potentially strengthen U.S.-Saudi relations if we are wise enough to seize that opportunity.

It is not U.S. influence that has encouraged these changes, in my view, but we should welcome and support them. The new leadership, as Simon said, includes Crown Prince Muhammad bin Nayef, the individual in charge of combating terrorism, and I can assure you that Saudis too focus on the need to retain Muhammad bin Nayef as the man that in their view has protected them from terrorism. There is not much concern about ISIS in Saudi Arabia, and the reason is Muhammad bin Nayef. From everything I hear cooperation with the U.S. on anti-terrorism is deemed to be good both on our side and theirs where he is concerned.

And to the extent that rich Saudis give money as do other rich people in the Persian Gulf to help finance terrorism, this does not, in my view, constitute official Saudi policy but rather evades it. They understand, whatever the case on 9/11, they understand now that terrorism is a threat to them too.

The new Deputy Crown Prince that Simon mentioned and the significance of both of these young men is that they are grandsons of the founder. So one is 55 and the Deputy Crown Prince is only 30. He is responsible for the country's defense, its economy, and Aramco. Literally, not since his grandfather Ibn Saud has a 30-year-old prince had the amount of power that he has. Last month he laid out what I think is a quite remarkable vision to sharply reduce dependence on oil; to create jobs for the 70 percent of the Saudi population that is under 30 years of age and many of them unemployed; to open opportunities for, as he put it, all Saudis which is a code word for including women; and he even on the record came out for ''more moderate brand of Islam.''

I stress this is a vision and not a plan, but having met with him myself in January in Riyadh, I do think that he is serious and I am happy to answer questions about that if you have any.

Mr. POE. Sum up your remarks, if you would, Ms. House.

Ms. HOUSE. Pardon. So I will skip Iran. I do not believe the Saudis are entirely paranoid when they look at what Iran is doing in the region, which is antithetical to their interests and I would argue to ours too.

So I will close by just saying it is not too late for a new U.S. administration to improve the relationship with Saudi Arabia, but it will require being honest about the fact that we don't have the same values, stressing a point the Ambassador made, and we do have a common strategic interest and that is a stable Persian Gulf that is free of any other hegemonic domination. And in my view we should seize this opportunity to support economic reform in Saudi Arabia and to rebuild trust with the Saudis by being honest about the difference, because instability in Saudi Arabia in a Middle East that is already completely unstable is in no one's interest. Thank you.

[The prepared statement of Ms. House follows:]

Chairman Poe, Congressman Keating, Members of the Subcommittee on Terrorism, Non-Proliferation and Trade:

Much is changing these days in Saudi Arabia. A new generation of young Saudi leaders now is in charge after nearly fifty years of rule by aged and increasingly infirm sons of Saudi founder, Ibn Saud. Also changing, unfortunately, is the longtime U.S.-Saudi relationship that has been built on a tacit understanding of Saudi oil for U.S. support and protection.

On my latest visit in January, the most recent of dozes of visits over the past nearly 40 years, I found Saudi royals and a growing number of citizens pointedly asking: Is the U.S. policy of avoiding involvement in Mideast problems permanent or will a new U.S. president once again exert traditional American leadership in the region and clear support for our Saudi ally? With the our presidential election some months in the future, it's impossible to know for sure what policy a new president will pursue. But I would argue it already is clear that the future of Saudi Arabia with a new generation of Al Saud leaders now in charge is and will be of critical importance to the U.S.

After all, Saudi Arabia is both the lynchpin of global oil supplies upon which the Western way of life still depends –and this despite increases in U.S. oil production--and it also is the wellspring of the rigid Wahhabi philosophy that motivates at least some of the jihadi hatred that seeks to destroy the western way of life. For these reasons, U.S. policy makers need to understand the forces at work inside the Kingdom as they seek to formulate U.S. policy toward the region. Support of Saudi stability and its oil exports and of Israeli democracy long have been paramount American interests in the region and, in my view, must remain so.

The new generation of leadership in Riyadh has at least a vision to transform the Saudi economy and to some extent its society in directions that will benefit not only Saudi citizens but also potentially strengthen U.S. –Saudi relations if we are wise enough to seize that opportunity. It is not waning U.S. influence that has encouraged these changes, but we should welcome and support them.

The new leadership includes Crown Prince Muhammad bin Nayef, also Minister of Interior and the individual in charge of combating terrorism—a cause we share with the Saudis. From everything I hear, cooperation with the U.S. on anti terrorism is strong and essential to maintain. To the extent individual rich Saudis, among others in Persian Gulf, are engaged in helping to finance terrorism this doesn't, in my view, constitute Saudi official policy but rather evades it.

The other new leader, Deputy Crown Prince Muhammad bin Salman, son of King Salman, is responsible for his country's defense and economy, including overseeing the national oil company ARAMCO. Not since Ibn Saud, who fought a 30-year civil war to subdue all Arabia to found the Kingdom of Saudi Arabia in 1932, has a 30-year-old prince had so much power. Last month the deputy crown prince laid out what for Saudi Arabia is a remarkable vision that includes privatizing much of the Saudi economy, sharply reducing dependence on oil, creating jobs for the many unemployed Saudi youth, opening opportunities for women, and even encouraging a more moderate brand of Islam.

At this stage this is a vision, with specific plans and then implementation to follow. What is different from previous promises of economic reform is that low oil prices are forcing change, and my conversation with Mohammed bin Salman in January convinces me there is a determined and highly energetic leader driving these changes. If only some of these changes take place, the young prince will be reversing generations of Saudi dependence on government and begun to make young Saudis more self-reliant. The traditional Saudi social contract has been loyalty for prosperity. In changing this contract one may ask whether a more self-reliant Saudi citizenry will maintain loyalty to the Al Saud. At this point the evidence is they will, if only because as they look around at their Middle East neighbors to see widespread chaos and carnage, the stability and security still provided by the Al Saud looks good by comparison.

Beyond domestic challenges, Saudi Arabia faces what it views as an existential threat from an expansionist Iran. This has relatively little to do with Iran's nuclear ambitions. The Saudis reluctantly and tepidly went along with President Obama's Iran nuclear deal. Much more alarming to the Saudis is Iranian mischief making on all of its borders from Iraq to Syria to Yemen and beyond. The Saudi-Iran rivalry is often defined as a religious one—Sunni vs Shia. More than that, however, it is a power struggle between the Persian Gulf's two leading nation states. In my view there is nothing paranoid about the Saudi fear of Iran, which has openly proclaimed its intent to topple the Al Saud and is busily expanding its regional influence at the expense of Saudi Arabia and the U.S. Not surprisingly, the Saudis see Iran as a far greater threat and more clear and present danger than ISIS even though they are willing to cooperate with the U.S. and others to confront ISIS.

It is not helpful to the Saudis, nor to the U. S., for the Obama administration to call the Saudis "free riders" and then add injury to insult by asking them to "learn to share" the neighborhood with Iran. It is as if we asked an American homeowner to share his backyard with criminals seeking to ransack and occupy his home. That is the way the Saudis see it and on this they are right.

It isn't too late for a new American administration of whichever party to explore improving relations with Saudi Arabia. The Saudis I've talked to including those in charge of the Kingdom still want a close relationship with the U.S. Their more assertive conduct of the past year results at least in part from a profound lack of trust in the current administration and thus the sense they must be prepared to protect their interests. The U.S. has an opportunity to work with these young princes clearly supported by King Salman to deepen cooperation against terrorism by both ISIS and Iran and to support economic and social reform in the Kingdom that the U.S. has long advocated. We don't have identical values with Saudi Arabia but we do share a common strategic interest—a Persian Gulf that is stable and free of any hegemonic domination. We should seize this opportunity to support reform and rebuild trust between our two countries because instability in Saudi Arabia is in no one's interest. In sum, Saudi Arabia is far from a perfect society but it is hard for me to imagine that either the Saudi people or Americans would be better off if the Al Saud were replaced by a pro Iranian regime like Assad, by ISIS or a Sunni theocracy or by chaos.

I thank the Chairman and his colleagues for this opportunity and look forward to answering your questions.

Mr. POE. Dr. Byman.

STATEMENT OF DANIEL L. BYMAN, PH.D., PROFESSOR, EDMUND A. WALSH SCHOOL OF FOREIGN SERVICE, GEORGETOWN UNIVERSITY

Mr. BYMAN. Chairman Poe, Ranking Member Keating, and members of this distinguished subcommittee, thank you for this opportunity to appear before you again and testify today.

Saudi Arabia has made considerable progress on counterterrorism in the last 15 years, but it still has a long way to go. Before the September 11th, 2001 terrorist attacks and, really, until al-Qaeda began to attack the kingdom directly in May 2003, Saudi Arabia was often uncooperative on counterterrorism. The Khobar Towers investigation often encountered significant problems working with the Saudi Government; al-Qaeda-linked individuals were often not investigated or at least those investigations were not shared with U.S. officials; and more broadly, individuals in Saudi Arabia, some of them linked to the government, supported an array of causes linked to Kashmir, Afghanistan and elsewhere, causes on which al-Qaeda also drew.

Since 2003, as others have said, there has been a tremendous change. Al-Qaeda brought the war home to Saudi Arabia and Saudi Arabia responded very strongly to the point where the 9/11 Commission declared in 2004 that the kingdom of Saudi Arabia is now locked in mortal combat with al-Qaeda. We have seen an aggressive effort to disrupt cells and also some progress on terrorism financing. We have seen intelligence sharing and significant penetrations, Saudi Arabia has served as a drone base for operations in Yemen, and this is invaluable.

The Islamic State, like al-Qaeda, is considered a top security threat by the Saudi regime. The Islamic State itself has declared Saudi Arabia to be an enemy, and its propaganda shows a black flag flying above Mecca. Islamic State terrorists have attacked mosques of Shia Muslims in the kingdom and also Saudi security officials, and the Saudi Government has arrested over 1,000 suspected Islamic State supporters, foiled several attacks, and is trying to take effort to stop people from traveling to fight.

Complicating this picture, however, is that support for terrorism in Saudi Arabia is often difficult to distinguish between the government, important organizations within society, and individuals acting against the will of the government. The Saudi regime's legitimacy is tied directly to the clerical establishment and since, really, the 1970s and perhaps before has been deeply engaged in supporting an array of Islamic causes around the world.

It has spent tens of billions of dollars on this, and as Ambassador Roemer mentioned, the article in the New York Times on Bosnia is almost a classic example of the sort of support we see where the Saudi Government was supporting an array of mosques and other institutions that fostered extremist teachings.

At times the regime has supported these institutions, at times it has deliberately ignored them, at other times it has cracked down so there has not been a single consistent response. And because these figures are often important for regime legitimacy, it is politically very difficult for them to do so.

We still see support for a number of radical groups around the world. I would single out Pakistan in particular as a place where this is still commonplace. The campaign in Yemen against the Houthis there has indirectly aided al-Qaeda in the Arabian Peninsula by giving them free space in which to operate.

Now the good news is, senior Saudi preachers working with the government have urged individuals not to go to terrorist groups, not to fight in Iraq and Syria, but as has been mentioned we see many preachers, many religious institutions condemning other Muslims in particular, also being very critical of non-Muslims and at times quite anti-American. And much of this in the United States at least would be free speech, right. It is not speech I like, but it would be free speech.

But nevertheless, it creates a fertile soil around the world of indoctrination and it plays directly into the narrative that the Islamic State pushes that it is defending true Islam against a host of enemies including many within the Muslim world.

I will conclude simply by saying that the United States has very deep differences with Saudi Arabia. These involve for example women's rights, homosexuality, religious freedom, freedom of speech—these are deep and fundamental differences. At the same time, Saudi Arabia is a vital partner on counterterrorism. And one of the difficulties in any policy is walking this line between a vital partner yet one who is more partner than friend. Thank you, Mr. Chairman.

[The prepared statement of Mr. Byman follows:]

The U.S.-SAUDI ARABIA COUNTETERRORISM RELATIONSHIP

Prepared Testimony of Daniel Byman

Professor and Senior Associate Dean, Edmund A. Walsh School of Foreign Service at
Georgetown University

Director of Research, Center for Middle East Policy at the Brookings Institution

House Committee on Foreign Affairs
Subcommittee on Terrorism, Nonproliferation, and Trade

May 24, 2016

Chairman Poe, Ranking Member Keating, members of this distinguished
subcommittee, and subcommittee staff, thank you for the opportunity to appear again
before you and testify today.

Saudi Arabia represents a paradox for U.S. counterterrorism. On the one hand, the
Saudi government is a close partner of the United States on counterterrorism. On the
other hand, Saudi support for an array of preachers and non-government organizations
contributes to an overall climate of radicalization, making it far harder to counter violent
extremism. Both these problems are manifest today as the United States seeks to counter
the Islamic State and its allies.

I argue that Saudi Arabia has made considerable progress on counterterrorism in
the last 15 years but still has a long way to go. Before the September 11, 2001 terrorist
attacks, and really until Al Qaeda began to attack the Kingdom directly in May 2003,
Saudi Arabia was often uncooperative on counterterrorism and more part of the problem
than part of the solution. Since 2003, the Saudi regime has emerged as a vital
counterterrorism partner, and several important successes against Al Qaeda in particular
are due in large part to Saudi cooperation. Complicating this picture, however, is that
much of Saudi 'support' for terrorism involves actors outside the Saudi government: the
regime has at times supported, at times deliberately ignored, and at still other times
cracked down on these actors. Some of these figures are important for regime legitimacy,
and it is difficult for the regime to openly oppose them. As a result, the Saudi Kingdom
still spews out material that is anti-Semitic, sectarian, glorifies several conflicts in which
jihadists play an active role, and otherwise contributes to a climate of radicalization.

Washington's ability to influence the Kingdom is limited, however, given the
Saudi domestic sensitivities of these issues. In the end, policymakers would do well to

remember that Saudi Arabia is a key partner but not a friend: the United States and Saudi Arabia share many common interests, but they do not share common values or a common worldview.

My testimony today first briefly reviews the U.S-Saudi relationship with regard to counterterrorism. I then highlight several key distinctions that are often missed when Saudi support for terrorism is examined. I then follow this examination by discussing the motivations behind Saudi Arabia's policies and conclude my testimony with some observations on the limits of U.S. influence.

Saudi Arabia's Troubled Past

Saudi Arabia has always been a conservative Muslim country, but when the Kingdom assumed its modern form in 1932 its religious energy was initially focused inward. In the 1960s, however, King Faysal bin Abdel-Aziz sought to form alliances based on a shared Muslim identity. A religious identity was meant to counter the radical pan-Arabism of Egyptian leader Gamal Abdel Nasser that was then threatening the legitimacy of monarchies throughout the Arab world. Such an identity would also unite states against international communism, which Faysal and the Saudi leadership vehemently opposed, and support Palestinian independence. Domestic politics also played a role: Faysal had essentially usurped the throne from his inept brother Saud, and support from the religious establishment was vital to ensuring his legitimacy.[1] To this end, Faysal created the Organization of the Islamic Conference and the Muslim World League and otherwise embraced an array of religious causes abroad.

The oil price surge after the 1973 war between Israel and its neighbors, and the resulting oil embargo and production cutback, enabled Saudi Arabia to contribute massive amounts to Islamic causes around the world. In the decades that followed, Faysal's successor as king, his brother Fahd, supported the building of mosques, Islamic centers and schools "by the thousands around the world."[2] His website claims that Saudi scholars helped create and administer 200 Islamic colleges, 210 Islamic centers, 1,500 mosques and 2,000 schools for Muslim children in non-Muslim countries.[3] Senior Treasury Department official David Aufhauser put the total figure for spending on these causes at "north of $75 billion."[4]

Much of this religious teaching and proselytizing was done outside the Saudi state by various charities that educated, provided health care, and otherwise offered services as part of their mission. A European Parliament report claimed the Saudis spent $10 billion to promote Salafism, the austere and puritanical version of Islam often referred to as "Wahhabism" after an important Saudi preacher, through charities like the Muslim World League, International Islamic Relief Organization, the al-Haramain Foundation, the

[1] Bruce Riedel, "Saudi Arabia is part of the problem and part of the solution to global jihad," *Markaz*, November 20, 2015, http://www.brookings.edu/blogs/markaz/posts/2015/11/20-clinton-saudi-arabia-riedel.
[2] John L. Esposito, "US Eyes Money Trails of Saudi-Backed Charities," *Washington Post*, August 19, 2004, http://www.washingtonpost.com/wp-dyn/articles/A13266-2004Aug18_2.html.
[3] Esposito, "US Eyes Money Trails of Saudi-Backed Charities."
[4] David Aufhauser, "An Assessment of Current Efforts to Combat Terrorism Financing," *Testimony of Hon. David D Aufhauser* (Government Printing Office: June 15, 2004), 46.

Medical Emergency Relief Charity, and the World Assembly of Muslim Youth.[5] Some of these charities were linked to terrorist groups like Al Qaeda and became an important part of the organization, particularly before 9/11. The Muslim World League reportedly funded training camps and religious schools in Pakistan and Afghanistan, exposing Afghans, Pakistanis, and foreigners to extremist ideologies. Al Haramain had a presence in roughly 50 countries and spent tens of millions: most went to proselytizing and humanitarian work, but some went to jihadist networks.[6]

The Kingdom in general was often slow to recognize the threat of terrorism and reluctant to cooperate with the United States. After the 1996 Khobar Towers bombing, the Saudi government did not share vital information with U.S. intelligence. Many of the causes linked to the global jihadist movement, like the fighting in Kashmir and Chechnya, enjoyed wide legitimacy within the Kingdom, and citizen support for these conflicts seemed to pose no direct threat to Saudi security. The Interior Minister in the 1990s, Nayef bin Abdelaziz (the father of the current crown prince) believed Bin Laden's terrorist reputation was a product of U.S. propaganda, and after 9/11 initially blamed the attacks on a "Zionist plot."[7]

The 2003 Turning Point

Much changed in 2003, when Al Qaeda began to attack the Kingdom directly, targeting expatriates there and also security forces. This led to a sustained terrorism campaign that claimed over a hundred lives and hundreds more injured between 2003 and 2006.[8] The current Crown Prince led the campaign against Al Qaeda, ultimately devastating its organization in the Kingdom. As a result of these attacks, the Kingdom embraced intelligence cooperation with the United States and began to see Al Qaeda as a deadly threat. Writing in 2004, the 9/11 Commission declared, "The Kingdom of Saudi Arabia is now locked in mortal combat with al Qaeda."[9]

[5] Policy Department, "The Involvement of Salafism/Wahhabism in Support and Supply and Arms to Rebel Groups Around the World," *Directorate-General For External Policies of the Union*, 2013, 5.
[6] Ahmed Rashid, *Taliban: Militant Islam, Oil, and Fundamentalism in Central Asia* (Cambridge: Yale University Press, 2000), 130; Bootie Cosgrove-Mather, "Al Qaeda Skimming Charity Money," *CBS News*, June 7, 2004, http://www.cbsnews.com/news/al-qaeda-skimming-charity-money/; "Protecting Charitable Organizations," Department of Treasury Database, 2002, https://www.treasury.gov/resource-center/terrorist-illicit-finance/Pageting-charities_execorder_13224-a.aspx#ahindo; National Commission on Terrorist Attacks upon the United States, *Monograph on Terrorism Financing* (New York: 2004), http://govinfo.library.unt.edu/911/staff_statements/911_TerrFin_Monograph.pdf.
[7] Bruce Riedel, "The Prince of Counterterrorism," *The Brookings Essay*, September 29, 2015, http://www.brookings.edu/research/essays/2015/the-prince-of-counterterrorism.
[8] Global Terrorism Database, *Study of Terrorism and Response to Terrorism (START)*, accessed May 16, 2016, http://apps.start.umd.edu/gtd/search/Results.aspx?charttype=line&chart=fatalities&casualties_type=&casualties_max=&country=173&count=100; RAND Database of Worldwide Terrorism Incidents, *RAND Corporation*, accessed May 16, 2016, http://smapp.rand.org/rwtid/search_form.php; Terrorism Index, *Institute for Economics & Peace*, accessed May 16, 2016, http://www.visionofhumanity.org/#page/indexes/terrorism-index/2003/SAU/OVER
[9] National Commission on Terrorist Attacks upon the United States, *The 9/11 Commission Report: Final Report of the National Commission on Terrorist Attacks upon the United States* (New York: 2004), 373.

Indicative of this change, in 2008 the United States and Saudi Arabia signed a bilateral agreement on technical counterterrorism cooperation. Under the agreement, the United States provides advisors, funded by Saudi Arabia, to assist on security measures. The U.S. military also assists in training Saudi forces.[10]

Saudi officials are now vital counterterrorism allies. They are playing a leading role in trying to stop funding to the Islamic State and the Al Qaeda core.[11] The shift in the Saudi approach and the importance of Saudi Arabia's role in counterterrorism can be seen in several successes against Al Qaeda's affiliate in Yemen, Al Qaeda in the Arabian Peninsula (AQAP). One of the more notable examples of Saudi Arabia's increasingly important role in combatting terrorism was the foiled 2010 AQAP cargo plane bomb plot. According to a story in the *New York Times*, Saudi intelligence provided the critical tipoff to the American and European intelligence officials that allowed British and Emirati security personnel to intercept the expertly concealed bombs that were already en route to the United States.[12] The last minute intelligence was the product of long-running Saudi intelligence operations to infiltrate AQAP.[13] The Saudi connection was probably decisive as the concealed explosives had already cleared multiple security screenings before the timely Saudi warning initiated the successful multilateral worldwide search.[14] In addition to these human intelligence capabilities within jihadist circles (not easily matched by Western intelligence), Saudi Arabia also plays a central role in the U.S. campaign against AQAP in Yemen by hosting a base for drone and other attacks in Yemen according to the BBC.[15]

The Islamic State, like Al Qaeda, is also considered a top security threat by the Saudi regime. The Islamic State has declared Saudi Arabia to be its enemy, and its propaganda shows its black flag flying above Mecca. Islamic State terrorists have attacked Shi'a Muslim mosques in the Kingdom and Saudi security officials. The Islamic State also called on Saudi subjects to assassinate senior Saudi leaders. More broadly, the Islamic State threatens the regime's legitimacy, claiming that it – rather than the Kingdom – is the true embodiment of a state under God's law. It has called the royal family "slaves of the Crusaders and allies of the Jews" and derided them for abandoning Muslims around the world.[16]

The Saudi government response to the Islamic State has been strong. The government has taken steps to stop Saudis from travelling abroad to support the Islamic State and other groups, including the arrest of those who traveled abroad to fight with radical groups. In addition, it has arrested more than 1,600 suspected Islamic State

[10] Christopher M. Blanchard, "Saudi Arabia: Background and U.S. Relations," Congressional Research Service, February 12, 2014, 18.

[11] Riedel, "Saudi Arabia is part of the problem and part of the solution to global jihad."

[12] Mark Mazzetti and Robert Worth, "U.S. Sees Complexity of Bombs as Link to Al Qaeda," *New York Times*, October 30, 2010, http://www.nytimes.com/2010/10/31/world/31terror.html.

[13] Julian Borger, Tom Finn, and Chris McGreal, "Cargo plane bomb plot: Saudi double agent 'gave crucial alert,'" *The Guardian*, November 1, 2010, http://www.theguardian.com/world/2010/nov/01/cargo-plane-plot-saudi-agent-gave-alert.

[14] Eric Schmitt and Scott Shane, "Saudis Warned U.S. of Attack Before Parcel Bomb Plot," *New York Times*, November 5, 2010, http://www.nytimes.com/2010/11/06/world/middleeast/06terror.html.

[15] "CIA operating drone base in Saudi Arabia, US media reveal," *BBC News*, February 6, 2013, http://www.bbc.com/news/world-middle-east-21350437.

[16] Blanchard, "Saudi Arabia," 12-13.

supporters in the Kingdom and reportedly foiled several attacks.[17] U.S. Treasury officials have declared the Saudis see "eye to eye" with the United States in stopping Islamic State fundraising, and the Kingdom has stepped up its monitoring of social media.[18] Senior religious officials with close ties to the royal family have also denounced the Islamic State (and Al Qaeda).[19] The Kingdom announced it was forming an "Islamic" military alliance, headquartered in Saudi Arabia, to fight terrorism.

The Kingdom has grown far more effective in stopping terrorist financing. Al Qaeda long drew on financial supporters in the Kingdom, and the Saudi government's capacity for stopping this was initially poor even after it began to go after the problem seriously.[20] (Part of the problem was that the Kingdom did not have an elaborate taxation system, so the government lacked knowledge of how much money its citizens had or how they spent it). The Kingdom invested heavily in fighting terrorist financing with considerable U.S. help. As a result, it is far harder to send money to terrorist groups from Saudi Arabia. In 2014, money going to fighters in Syria was often channeled via Kuwait to avoid Saudi countermeasures.[21] Despite these more aggressive measures and considerable progress, financial support for Sunni extremist groups from Saudis remains a significant problem.[22] Groups in Pakistan and elsewhere often benefit from the support of wealthy Saudis, and it is not clear how hard the Saudi government is trying to stop these flows.

Saudi Arabia also has initiated a terrorist rehabilitation program. This well-funded program gives terrorists a chance to reintegrate into Saudi society. Religious leaders are involved to dissuade participants from radical views. Participants also receive a job and family support. Some of those who have gone through the program, however, have returned to extremism, including several important members of AQAP.[23]

Considerable problems remain. As former senior CIA official Bruce Riedel contends, "Saudi sources remain major funders of groups like the Afghan Taliban and Lashkar-e Taiba in Pakistan. Some accounts suggest Saudi money has gone to al-Qaida's affiliate in Syria, the al-Nusra Front."[24] Although Riyadh opposes the Islamic State, it sees the Syrian regime, with its close ties to Iran, as a far greater danger and has focused its energies accordingly. Despite greater regime efforts to reduce the flow of fighters

[17] Ibid., 11-12.
[18] Lori Plotkin Boghardt, "Saudi Funding of ISIS," *The Washington Institute for Near East Policy*, June 23, 2014, http://www.washingtoninstitute.org/policy-analysis/view/saudi-funding-of-isis; Maria Abi-Habib and Rory Jones, "Kuwait Attack Renews Scrutiny of Terror Support Within Gulf States," *Wall Street Journal*, June 28, 2015, http://www.wsj.com/articles/kuwait-attack-renews-scrutiny-of-terror-support-within-gulf-states-1435529549.
[19] "Saudi Grand Mufti Issues Statement Saying ISIL, Al-Qa'ida Are 'Khawarij,'" *Al Sharq* (Dammam), August 19, 2014.
[20] For a comprehensive review, see National Commission on Terrorist Attacks upon the United States, Monograph on Terrorism Financing (New York: 2004), http://govinfo.library.unt.edu/911/staff_statements/911_TerrFin_Monograph.pdf.
[21] Boghardt, "Saudi Funding of ISIS;" Abi-Habib and Jones, "Kuwait Attack Renews Scrutiny of Terror Support Within Gulf States."
[22] U.S. Department of State, *Country Reports on Terrorism 2014* (2015).
[23] Abi-Habib and Jones, "Kuwait Attack Renews Scrutiny of Terror Support Within Gulf States."
[24] Riedel, "Saudi Arabia is part of the problem and part of the solution to global jihad." See also Yaroslav Trofimov, "To U.S. Allies, Al Qaeda Affiliate in Syria Becomes the Lesser Evil," *Wall Street Journal*, June 11, 2015, http://www.wsj.com/articles/to-u-s-allies-al-qaeda-affiliate-in-syria-becomes-the-lesser-evil-1434022017.

abroad, Saudis still have found it easy to travel and fight on behalf of the Islamic State – they are perhaps the largest source of foreign fighters for the group.[25]

Perhaps most important, Saudi Arabia is home to many preachers and religious organizations that embrace sectarianism and oppose a U.S. role in the Middle East. A number of prominent Saudi preachers regularly condemn Shi'a Muslims, thus validating the Islamic State's sectarian campaign and otherwise increasing its legitimacy. Some also blame the United States for a host of ills, embracing conspiracy theories such as the Bush administration being behind the 9/11 attacks. There is relative progress, however, in that many senior religious leaders do urge Saudis not to be foreign fighters or otherwise participate in conflicts abroad, arguing instead that local Muslims or state authorities should be the ones to respond.[26]

Saudi Arabia considers Al Qaeda to be a mortal enemy, yet its military campaign in Yemen has indirectly assisted the group. By targeting and pushing back the Houthis in Yemen, which Riyadh considers (largely erroneously) to be a pawn of Tehran, Saudi Arabia has given breathing space to AQAP, which also is fighting the Houthis. Recently, however, Saudi-backed forces have focused on AQAP as well as the Houthis, forcing AQAP to retreat in several areas.[27]

Key Distinctions

Understanding Saudi Arabia's relationship with terrorists, however, is far more difficult than assessing Iran's backing of terrorism, which is open, extensive, and state-sponsored.[28] Much of Saudi support is done by non-state actors. Yet being 'non-state' does not absolve the Saudi government of responsibility. These non-state actors enjoy a range of relationships to the Saudi regime. Some receive or did receive official patronage. Others, particularly those tied to leading clerics in the Kingdom, are embraced indirectly by the regime's self-proclaimed role as Defender of the Faithful. And still others are truly private, acting independently of the government and in times in opposition to it.

In addition, the Saudi royal family itself occupies an unusual role. In one sense the royal family, with its tens of thousands of princes, is not the government. However,

[25] The Soufan Group, *Foreign Fighters*, December 2015, http://soufangroup.com/wp-content/uploads/2015/12/TSG_ForeignFightersUpdate3.pdf.

[26] "Saudi Arabia's clerics condemn IS but preach intolerance," *Reuters*, September 10, 2014, http://www.reuters.com/article/us-saudi-islam-security-idUSKBN0H501E20140910; *The Week* Staff, "How Saudi Arabia exports radical Islam," *The Week*, August 8, 2015, http://theweek.com/articles/570297/how-saudi-arabia-exports-radical-islam; Victor Mallet, "Madrassas: behind closed doors," *Financial Times Magazine* (October 30, 2015), http://on.ft.com/1WoRqVT.

[27] Thomas Joscelyn, "AQAP says it withdrew from Mukalla to protect resident," *The Long War Journal*, May 1, 2016, http://www.longwarjournal.org/archives/2016/05/aqap-says-it-withdrew-from-mukalla-to-protect-residents.php; Bruce Riedel, "What the Yemen ceasefire means for the Gulf, the anti-ISIS campaign, and U.S. security," *Markaz*, April 12, 2016, http://www.brookings.edu/blogs/markaz/posts/2016/04/12-yemen-ceasefire-us-security-riedel; Yara Bayoumy, Noah Browning, and Mohammed Ghobari, "How Saudi Arabia's war in Yemen has made al Qaeda stronger – and richer," *Reuters*, April 8, 2015, http://www.reuters.com/investigates/special-report/yemen-aqap/; Bruce Riedel, "Al-Qaida's Hadramawt emirate," *Markaz*, July 12, 2015, http://www.brookings.edu/blogs/markaz/posts/2015/07/12-al-qaeda-yemen-emirate-saudi-riedel.

[28] For my broader thoughts on state support, see Daniel Byman, *Deadly Connections: States that Sponsor Terrorism* (Cambridge University Press, 2005).

the family's and the government's finances are interwoven, and if a prince supports a group it has an unofficial imprimatur of approval. King Salman himself, for example, helped raise money for the *mujahedin* in Afghanistan and the Balkans.[29]

Many of these voices are responsible for indoctrination rather than direct violence. That is to say that might propagate views on the Satanic nature of Jews, the apostasy of Shia or the heretical nature of the Ahmadiyyas, and the legitimacy of using violence to fight foreign occupiers of Muslim lands, be it Indian forces in Kashmir, U.S. forces in Iraq, or Israeli forces in historic Palestine.[30] Such support, in the United States, would often be considered distasteful but part of protected free speech. For terrorists, however, it can prove invaluable as it provides theological legitimacy for their actions, enabling them to attract recruits and funds.

Motivations

Saudi counterterrorism policy represents a mix of ideology, domestic politics, and cold pragmatism.

Most Saudis, including many in the government, are strong supporters of an austere version of Salafism, regard non-Muslims (and most non-Salafis) as hostile, and see fighting Israel, India, and at times even the United States as legitimate. Missionary work, such as spreading 'true' Islam through preaching and education, is particularly supported across a wide spectrum of the population.

For the royal family, this general domestic support is mixed with a need for legitimacy. The royal family is not elected, and its record of providing services and economic growth is mixed. It is particularly vulnerable now given the collapse of the price of oil since mid-2014: the Kingdom's budget deficit today is the largest in its history.[31] As such, the royal family relies heavily on its pact with the clerical establishment to implement Islamic law in the Kingdom and to defend the faith in general. Rejecting missionary work an religious education, with this pact in mind, is difficult, and even rejecting violence in the name of the faith is hard if the cause is popular, as is the anti-Assad struggle in Syria today. The new king, Salman bin Abdel Aziz Al Saud, if anything, has moved closer to the clerical establishment since he took power in 2015. He fired the Kingdom's only female Cabinet minister and is in regular contact with leading conservative clerics.[32]

The Saudi royal family, however, is also pragmatic. It values its relationship with the United States, and the 2003 attacks taught it that problems that are seemingly safely abroad can come home quickly and unexpectedly. So the time-honored practice of

---

[29] Scott Shane, "Moussaoui Calls Saudi Princes Patrons of Al Qaeda," *New York Times*, February 3, 2015, http://www.nytimes.com/2015/02/04/us/zacarias-moussaoui-calls-saudi-princes-patrons-of-al-qaeda.html; Bruce Riedel, "The Next King of the Saudis: Salman, the Family Sheriff," *The Daily Beast*, January 23, 2015, http://www.thedailybeast.com/articles/2015/01/22/the-next-king-of-the-saudis-salman-the-family-sheriff.html; David Andrew Weinberg, "King Salman's Shady History," *Foreign Policy*, January 27, 2015, http://foreignpolicy.com/2015/01/27/king-salmans-shady-history-saudi-arabia-jihadi-ties/

[30] Michael Scott Doran, "The Saudi Paradox," *Foreign Affairs* 83, no. 1 (January/February 2004), https://www.foreignaffairs.com/articles/saudi-arabia/2004-01-01/saudi-paradox.

[31] Bruce Riedel, "Saudi Arabia's Mounting Security Problems," *Al-Monitor*, December 28, 2015, http://www.al-monitor.com/pulse/originals/2015/12/saudi-yemen-security-salman-houthi-gulf.html.

[32] Riedel, "The Prince of Counterterrorism."

diversion – convincing radicals to go after other targets – is risky. The regime is particularly sensitive to anything that might call into question the regime's legitimacy, and it has not hesitated to silence or imprison popular clerics when necessary.

A Changing Saudi Arabia?

Making these generalizations less certain, the Kingdom is now in the midst of a profound change. King Salman is the last of his generation: all future Saudi leaders (and the vast majority of Saudis) will have grown up in a Kingdom that has known considerable wealth. In the past two years the Kingdom, which historically preferred to act behind the scenes, has already charted an increasingly independent and assertive path. Salman has shaken up succession, gone to war in Yemen against initial U.S. opposition, openly criticized the Obama administration harshly on the Iran deal, stepped up action in Syria, and otherwise is playing a far more leading role in the region than is traditional. On counterterrorism, the appointment of Mohammad bin Nayef as Crown Prince is at least promising, as he is pro-American and an aggressive and effective foe of Al Qaeda and other groups.[33]

The Kingdom is also beginning – in rhetoric at least – a massive economic restructuring. The Kingdom's economy remains dependent on oil, its public sector is bloated, its education system need to teach more practical knowledge, and Saudis have grown used to massive government subsidies: all daunting challenges. The new King and his young son, the new Deputy Crown Prince, have proposed an ambitious set of reforms to wean the Kingdom off its dependence on oil. Possible changes include a decrease in subsidies, the sale of public lands, and a value added tax.[34] The Kingdom, however, is often glacial regarding the pace of any reforms. To the extent that the Kingdom's own radicalization problems are driven by economic and social ills, little progress is likely in the near-term, and things may get far worse.

Limits to U.S. Influence

U.S. pressure under the Bush and Obama administrations has moved Saudi Arabia away from many dangerous activities and has helped transform Saudi capacity in fighting terrorism. Even if the key motivation was the change in the perceived threat to the Kingdom itself rather than U.S. influence, these are considerable successes that deserve recognition.

Changing Saudi policy still further is difficult. Although the United States has sold the Kingdom almost $100 billion in arms during the Obama administration, the Saudi media remains critical of the President as unreliable and hostile to the Kingdom. Riyadh, moreover, is frustrated with U.S. policy regarding Iran in particular but also in the region in general. Saudi Arabia backed the coup in Egypt, in opposition to U.S. policy, and Saudi leaders were previously outraged that the United States abandoned the Mubarak regime. The Obama administration has largely abandoned criticizing the Saudi

---

[33] For an overview, see Riedel, "The Prince of Counterterrorism."
[34] Peter Waldman, "The $2 Trillion Project to Get Saudi Arabia's Economy Off Oil," *Bloomberg Businessweek*, April 21, 2016, http://www.bloomberg.com/news/features/2016-04-21/the-2-trillion-project-to-get-saudi-arabia-s-economy-off-oil; Blanchard, "Saudi Arabia," 8.

regime on human rights grounds, but it is important to remember that most Saudis do not share U.S. values regarding women's and homosexual rights, religious liberty, and other basic freedoms that are fundamental to American society.

Many issues regarding counterterrorism – particularly the promotion of extremism abroad via sectarianism and criticism of non-Muslims – touch on core domestic political issues vital to the regime's legitimacy and very survival. Change in these areas will at best be slow, and the United States should expect progress to end or even reverse should the regime's domestic situation face challenges.

Quiet pressure is almost always best when trying to change Saudi policy. The small circle of decision-makers in Saudi Arabia does not take well to public embarrassment, and they believe strongly in the value of close personal relationships. To be effective, U.S. pressure must involve top officials, including the President. Otherwise, it will simply be ignored or may even prove counterproductive.

Saudi Arabia is vital partner in the struggle to defeat the Islamic State, Al Qaeda, and other groups. But it is not a friend. Demonizing Saudi Arabia does not help advance U.S. interests, but nor should critics of U.S. policy in the region see Washington and Riyadh as fully aligned given the profound difference in values.

Mr. Poe. I thank all of our witnesses for their testimony, and I recognize myself for 5 minutes of questions. I will make this comment. It is obvious that Saudi Arabia acts in its own interest. Not necessarily that is a bad thing, but countries should act in their own best interest including the United States. We should act in our best interest.

Regarding the 9/11 Commission report, the 28 classified pages, I would like each of you just to give me a yes or no on this. Should those 28 pages be declassified in your opinion? Ambassador, you have already said.

Mr. Roemer. I am strongly in favor of declassifying the 28 pages as soon as possible, Mr. Chairman.

Mr. Poe. Mr. Henderson.

Mr. Henderson. Since you limit me to a yes or no answer, the answer is yes.

Mr. Poe. Thank you.

Ms. House.

Ms. House. As a journalist my answer is obviously yes.

Mr. Poe. And Dr. Byman.

Mr. Byman. Yes, Mr. Chairman.

Mr. Poe. As mentioned in your testimony, and many members have talked about JASTA and the Senate unanimously passing legislation last week, the bill doesn't mention any governments but it says that the bill makes a foreign government that provides tangible support to terrorists who carry out an attack on the United States subject to the jurisdiction of an American courts. Do you think that is a good idea, Ambassador?

Mr. Roemer. Mr. Chairman, I would put my former congressman hat on, but also try to talk a little about my hat as a former diplomat. I am also strongly in favor of the Senate bill. I think it is a bipartisan bill where Senator Cornyn, who you know well, and Senator Lindsey Graham have both put in their considerations and narrowed the scope of the bill so that it does not stretch across the world and create problems on sovereign immunity for other diplomatic situations. It is narrowed to this particular issue with Saudi Arabia.

And Mr. Chairman, I would then say that given that we are a country of rules and laws and that if our court thereby finds that there was some activity or action by Saudi that contributed, let our courts prevail and let justice prevail. We should pass this bill.

Mr. Poe. Thank you, Ambassador.

Mr. Henderson.

Mr. Henderson. I agree that our courts should be allowed to prevail with the caveat of be careful what you wish for and taking such action could lead to Saudi retaliation whether it be withdrawing Treasury bills or actions against Americans in the kingdom. I don't think that is what we are looking for.

Mr. Poe. Ms. House, what do you think, should we pass it or not? It is our decision that is going to come up next week. The Senate did it. What do you think?

Ms. House. This is beyond my expertise. But as someone who travels abroad a lot and in Saudi Arabia, a very closed and conservative society, I worry about what Simon just said, be careful, and what Congressman Issa raised earlier, the risk of retaliation.

I mean, I believe vengeance is mine sayeth the Lord, I shall repay; that perhaps there is something to be said for letting the Lord handle that part of the vengeance on the Saudis.

Mr. POE. All right.

Dr. Byman, can you narrow it down to a yes or no?

Mr. BYMAN. I will say a caveated yes, sir.

Mr. POE. We don't get to caveat vote. It is a yea or a nay without an explanation. I am just—what is your opinion of the bill?

Mr. BYMAN. My opinion of the bill is that as long as the bar is very high for what constitutes state support, then it is appropriate for the courts to decide this.

Mr. POE. A couple of other observations, this hearing, you all have talked about a lot of things including Iran, and the Saudis have a two-front war apparently or a two-front concern in the Middle East. It is terrorism and it is also Iran. And I think as Mr. Henderson testified that our concern really is terrorism and not so much Iran. The crimes in Syria have cost millions of folks to move into Europe. Has the Saudi Arabian Government ever taken any Syrian refugees into Saudi Arabia?

Mr. HENDERSON. My understanding is that Saudi Arabia along with the other Gulf states has not taken refugees in a manner that we would recognize; that Europe is taking refugees. I believe that at least some of the Gulf states, I am not sure if it applies to Saudi Arabia, have been generous in allowing Syrians who already live in their countries to bring in relatives and family members at this time.

Mr. POE. All right, thank you. I think it is somewhat interesting that Saudi Arabia does not take Syrian refugees, which is a whole different issue. I am going to yield to the ranking member from Massachusetts for his questions. Mr. Keating.

Mr. KEATING. Thank you, Mr. Chairman.

I wanted to see if you could comment on this. As Ambassador Roemer and Dr. Byman have mentioned there has been, you know, increases in legal reforms and efforts to really constrain financially the ability of people in Saudi Arabia to, you know, fund for this extremist activity.

Now how successful has that been, and if hasn't been as successful as it should be, then why not? Is it a lack of will or are they encountering difficulties just implementing this? If you could comment on that because I think it is a fundamental question of transparency. They are doing this. They are attempting to do it, how effective have they been?

Mr. ROEMER. I would say, Mr. Keating, I hate to sound like Harry Truman who talked about economists on the one hand and the other hand, but on the one hand you see the Saudis cooperating, helping us, cracking down on terrorism, passing national laws to try to restrict people from joining up with the Islamic State, and on the other hand as we read in the recent article in the New York Times, Saudi money and government financing for more jihadis going from Kosovo to Syria.

We need both the Saudi hands working together with the United States on counterterrorism as a principal concern along with our other strategic objectives, which are Middle East stability, which are making sure that Iran cannot do us harm through terrorism, through promoting human rights and through some of the other key issues that we have mentioned here.

I would also say, Mr. Keating, that our relationship with the Saudis, while it is difficult right now on this particular issue, we have had difficulties with them and they have had difficulties with us before. They were not in support of the U.S. invading Iraq in 2003. They were not in favor of the U.S. negotiating President Obama's nuclear deal and kicked back vociferously about that. They were not, you know, for Harry Truman recognizing Israel so quickly. So we can get through this, but I am glad that counterterrorism is front and center today.

Mr. KEATING. Dr. Byman, just quickly. Has it been effective and if not why?

Mr. BYMAN. It has been somewhat effective. We have seen groups in Chechnya run out of money because of a decrease in Saudi support. The Islamic State advised its supporters in the kingdom to channel money through Kuwait because the efforts in the kingdom were extensive enough to be disruptive.

But a number of causes still enjoy considerable domestic legitimacy. Again, I mentioned Pakistan. And as a result, you can give to groups that are kind of one level out from the most radical but the individuals involved often cross over. Part of it is simply technically very hard, but I think part of a problem is a deep political will issue to go after the entirety of the problem.

Mr. KEATING. Thank you. Just quickly, I think the panel has done a great job covering as time permits a wide array. But I want to ask you this question if you could just answer it briefly because of time, where do you see Saudi Arabia 10 years from now particularly in terms of the U.S.?

Mr. HENDERSON. Saudi Arabia in 10 years' time will, I think, be very much recognizable as the Saudi Arabia of today. I don't anticipate any revolution, any emerging republic to replace the royal family.

What I don't know is who will be king of Saudi Arabia then, when the transition will occur, and under what circumstances it will occur. This is very different from the way our knowledge of Saudi Arabia looking backwards over the last 30 or 40 years where there was a predictability to the whole thing. With the eminence, the increasing prominence of the 30-year-old Muhammad bin Salman, previous conceptions about how Saudi Arabia is going to move forward have to be discarded.

Mr. KEATING. So it is less predictable. Does anyone else quickly want to venture any vision?

Ms. HOUSE. It is definitely less predictable, but I think it is likely not to be dramatically different. But in my view it will have inched forward some. Women are, I know nobody likes to hear this, but they are much better educated than the men and they are much more willing to work and they are managing to get opportunities.

And the Saudi people, while unhappy with various things at home, look around at the total chaos and bloodshed in the rest of the Middle East and whatever they think of the Saudi royal family now, they prize stability over change.

Mr. KEATING. Thank you very much. I yield back.

Mr. POE. I thank the gentleman. Mr. Wilson, South Carolina.

Mr. WILSON. Thank you, Judge Poe.

And Ms. House, Saudi Arabia has incredible influence in the Islamic world. With the status of reforms to the Saudi educational curriculum promised in 2008, has that been produced or not?

Ms. HOUSE. No. I don't think so, because as the man who was in charge of changing the textbooks told me when I was writing my book, at some level it doesn't matter what the textbooks say. When you close the door, the teacher is in charge, and all too many of the teachers are in total agreement with the more rigid Wahhabi philosophy that has been ingrained.

Mr. WILSON. And it seems illogical to me the promotion of jihadism would create such a level of instability that would threaten the regime in Riyadh. Is that not correct?

Ms. HOUSE. No, they have been very successful. As I said, Muhammad bin Nayef, the Crown Prince, they have been very successful at controlling terrorism in the kingdom since the 2003, '04, '05 period when they had a lot of it. And now, and people want that stability and if repression occurs against some human rights advocates in the context of that most Saudis are sadly willing to overlook that. As Dr. Byman said, what we would call free speech they punish.

Mr. WILSON. And it just seems again counterproductive, but hope springs eternal.

Ms. HOUSE. Counterproductive to do what?

Mr. WILSON. To the existence of the kingdom. That there would be such an extremist ideology that just could——

Ms. HOUSE. No, as he said, it is fundamentally what gives the royal family their legitimacy is that we support the Wahhabis who are propagating the one true Islam. And they prefer that it be exported as they are doing in other places, and they control themselves, the jihadis, at home.

Mr. WILSON. Well, I just see the instability whether it be Yemen or you name it, or Pakistan or Libya, wherever, Kosovo. But bottom line, thank goodness we have good people like Ambassador Roemer around.

And Ambassador, I am really grateful. From the state of South Carolina, the late governor John C. West served as Ambassador to Saudi Arabia and worked very closely to establish a warm, bipartisan relationship. Can you judge the effectiveness of Saudi Arabia's attempt to fight terrorism financing? Have we seen a noticeable impact on their financing of groups in the region?

Mr. ROEMER. Congressman Wilson, thank you for the question. I would say that it is inconsistent on financial crackdowns and financial progress. We have probably seen since 2003 more progress from the Saudis than at any other time once they had the internal attacks and took this quite seriously.

But I think as Dan Byman said, we often see this supported, ignored, and then a crackdown, and supported, ignored and a crackdown, and not consistent enough. The financial area is somewhere where I think the United States and the Treasury Department has been very successful at working with the Saudi Government in some areas, but I don't think it is consistent enough and I don't think it has passed through from the top levels of Saudi society down into the cultural and religious areas.

Mr. WILSON. Well, thank goodness again that you are involved, and we need your guidance.

And Mr. Byman, how would you characterize the Saudi counter-terrorism campaign in Yemen? Has it been effective?

Mr. BYMAN. Sir, for the most part the campaign has not been effective. They have gone into Yemen primarily to fight the Houthi movement there which they believe is backed, is tied to Iran. In my view the ties are real, but the Saudis overstate them considerably.

But the Middle East, sir, as you know is a mess, and what makes it more confusing is the Houthis are fighting al-Qaeda in the Arabian Peninsula. So by fighting the group the Saudis believe is tied to Iran, they have given the al-Qaeda group more freedom of operation. Recently they have been trying to fight both, but that said, the big winner of the Saudi intervention has been al-Qaeda of the Arabian Peninsula.

Mr. WILSON. Well, again, thank each of you for as you say a very complicated situation. Thank you.

Mr. POE. The chair recognizes the gentleman from California, Mr. Sherman, for 5 minutes.

Mr. SHERMAN. Okay. Let me just quiz you all by a show of hands. How many of you believe that the House of Saud will be in control of Saudi Arabia 15 years from now, a monarchy under the House of Saud? If you think so, raise your hand.

Ms. HOUSE. 15.

Mr. SHERMAN. 15 years. Okay, we have got four hands raised. That is a better odds than many governments in the Middle East get.

Ms. HOUSE. People are passive.

Mr. SHERMAN. Second, the Saudis have said they would sell $750 billion of assets if we pass this law. I don't think they would do it, but even when they say they would do it is this to avoid attachment as a litigation defense strategy, or is this to punish and scare the United States? Why are they claiming to do the 750? Ambassador.

Mr. ROEMER. Congressman, I don't think they would do it. They didn't buy those securities in American bonds to do us a charitable work. They did it to make money. They are not going to sell it if it loses them a lot of money——

Mr. SHERMAN. On the other hand you could——

Mr. ROEMER [continuing]. Opening that threat to us. I don't think——

Mr. SHERMAN. You could say that a U.S. bond is four basis points better than investing in a euro bond, and then if there is a genuine risk that a lawsuit will lead to the attachment of those assets, because if there is a lawsuit I don't know whether the damages are only $1 billion. Maybe they are $10 billion. Maybe with punitives they are $750 billion. So I don't think they would do it to punish us. I wonder whether it is a litigation strategy.

Just some commentary, I mean, Saudi Arabia is a monarchy, so by definition you don't have the right of the people to control the government. So you can't have free speech because a lot of speakers would say that the people should control the government. And their human rights toward women, LGBT, and religious freedom is zero. Now we accept that. I mean, a Mormon missionary in Riyadh is,

I assume, a dead Mormon missionary or just an imprisoned Mormon missionary. I don't know which.

But, so I focus on, okay, we know that all about them. The question is are they exporting terrorism? Two ways that they can export terrorism, one is to the finance the people that actually blow things up. Here is the money today, blow something up tomorrow. 9/11 support, of course. That is the focus of the 28 pages. But the other is to finance a propaganda education machine designed to teach millions of people that blowing things up is a good idea.

The House of Saud and the Wahhabis have an alliance that goes back to the 1700s. I can't fault them if they finance efforts to say, hey, you should strictly follow Islam. Pray five times a day; don't slough off and do four. But we are not talking about just orthodox practice. We are talking about are they teaching people.

How much money is Saudi Arabia spending out of government money or royal money to spread Wahhabi Islam, and is there a form of Wahhabi Islam they can spread that is orthodox but not violent?

Mr. ROEMER. The answer to your first question is it doesn't matter much how much they are spending because it doesn't cost much. We found on the 9/11 Commission that the entire operation against the United States to pull off——

Mr. SHERMAN. Oh, yes. If they were financing the people that blow things up you do that for small amounts of money. But if your goal is to change popular opinion from Rubat to Jakarta and to create millions of people who think that killing non-Muslims is a good idea that can be expensive. And I know that others have talked about did they finance this or that terrorist attack. My focus is, are they financing a well designed propaganda effort to create millions of pro-terrorist thinkers? Does anybody have an idea how much they are spending to finance Wahhabism, and can you draw distinction between violent and non-violent Wahhabism or is there just one Wahhabism?

Ms. HOUSE. There are lots of Saudis who would argue that you can draw a distinction between violent and non-violent Wahhabism. The late King Abdullah fired some of the senior religious scholars who in essence the supreme court of what is the right Islam. King Salman has restored one of them. So there are a lot of people in Saudi Arabia who do not believe in killing other people.

But I think your point is well taken that it is more, in my view it is less the direct financing than the indirect promotion of a form of religion that we obviously would regard as intolerant.

Mr. SHERMAN. I would go beyond intolerant. I mean those who are just orthodox——

Ms. HOUSE. Intolerant and violent.

Mr. SHERMAN [continuing]. And say bad things, who teach that if you have, you know, you are going to hell if you have a ham sandwich, that is a certain intolerance. It is when you start advocating blowing things up that I draw the line. I yield back.

Mr. POE. I thank the gentleman. The chair recognizes the gentleman from Pennsylvania, Mr. Perry.

Mr. PERRY. Thanks, Mr. Chairman. To my good friend from California, according to a Senate Judiciary Committee testimony, Saudi

Arabia spends $4 billion a year on mosques, madrassa preachers, students, and textbooks to spread the Wahhabi creed, if that helps out at all.

If I could turn to Mr. Henderson, do you think that the kingdom, the House of Saud, can survive without its affiliation to Wahhabism? Can it survive?

Mr. HENDERSON. Could you just repeat the question?

Mr. PERRY. Can the kingdom, can the House of Saud survive without its affiliation to Wahhabism?

Mr. HENDERSON. It would be a very different kingdom. Historically, it is a partnership between the House of Saud and the religious leadership.

Mr. PERRY. So is that a tepid yes? Is it, I mean so you are saying there is a chance? What is that?

Mr. HENDERSON. I don't think—it is a hypothetical which I——

Mr. PERRY. Well, I guess——

Mr. HENDERSON [continuing]. Never thought of it before and because I don't think it is within the range of realistic possibility.

Mr. PERRY. Okay, so it is not realistic. Because it seems to me the House of Saud, the Saudis have said we are now an unreliable partner, so to speak, because we are not able to protect their monarchy.

But I would say that they have been duplicitous and unreliable because they have spent $4 billion a year or something to that effect to spread Wahhabism around the globe, including North America, et cetera. I mean, I have got all the stats here of the thousands of mosques and centers and colleges and, you know, 80 percent of the mosques, 1,200 mosques operating in the U.S. were constructed after 2001, mostly with Saudi financing. And it just goes on and on from there whether you go to Europe or wherever you go.

That having been said, at some point as an ally, who we are engaged in this war on terrorism whether we like it or not because the war has come to our doorstep, is it too much to ask, I guess that is the question. Is it too much to ask for them to stop that? To stop it.

Mr. HENDERSON. I think what you are describing is a very valid question. I did not recognize comments of your colleague Mr. Sherman in terms of defining what is journalistically known as Wahhabism as being necessarily violent. I think it is intolerant and it is a conservative and strict Islam which is——

Mr. PERRY. I would rather you not use the term "conservative" as opposed to fundamentalist. Thank you very kindly.

Mr. HENDERSON. Sorry, it is the British-ness in me. I am sorry.

Mr. PERRY. I appreciate that but it means something here.

Mr. HENDERSON. Forgive me.

Mr. SHERMAN. With a personal approvance, I would prefer you go back to the original phraseology.

Mr. PERRY. Reclaiming my time and then some, Mr. Chairman.

Mr. HENDERSON. Okay. I think there is a concern amongst leaders of Muslim communities in other parts of the world that Saudi Arabia spends a lot of money bringing mosques and bringing teachers to their countries and introducing a stricter form of Islam to——

44

Mr. PERRY. But do they not make the connection that when they bring the mosques and the teachers and the teaching they are bringing terrorism, an ideology of terrorism and death?

Mr. HENDERSON. I don't think Wahhabism has an ideology of terrorism.

Mr. PERRY. Okay, I appreciate your opinion.

Ms. House, you talked about our relationship with the Saudis and Israel and how important it is to maintain that stability in the Middle East, but does that mean that the United States should accept the circumstances of what many Americans, myself included, see as Saudi Arabia support, material support, through the construction of mosques and the ideology around the world including their own neighborhood, should we accept that for the stability, as you put it, in our relationship with Israel and Saudi Arabia?

Ms. HOUSE. Well, I think we ought to, and hopefully we do, continuously try to underscore to them that it is not in——

Mr. PERRY. Ma'am, with all due respect this has been going on for decades. At what point do we require action on their part? Talking is one thing, but there are terrorists running around the globe——

Ms. HOUSE. Well, what kind of action can you require?

Mr. PERRY. Well, we can request that they no longer fund this; that they change the teaching; that they get in the game on this like we have to be. Is that too much to ask? And is it worth the stability?

Ms. HOUSE. It is not too much to ask, but I don't know that it will result in a change.

Mr. PERRY. Is it too much to demand for the sake of our relationship?

Ms. HOUSE. Well, what is the rest of the demand? If not, we are not going to protect our interest in the Persian Gulf anymore?

Mr. PERRY. What about our interest in our schools and our neighborhoods here where people are going to blow us up? What about those interests, or are they not important? Because they are coming here, they are here now.

Ms. HOUSE. They are.

Mr. PERRY. So at what point, what is the tipping point, if you know?

Ms. HOUSE. I just think—I didn't get to talk about Iran. I think that you are focused on Saudi Arabia today for obvious reasons, but they are not the only people propagating terrorism in the Middle East. Iran is too.

Mr. PERRY. Okay, I agree with that. But for their part, let's just talk their part and our relationship. Do we just continue to accept it without any—there is no benchmark. We don't see any milestones at all from my standpoint.

Mr. POE. The witness can answer that question.

Ms. HOUSE. I think it is my personal view that the regime could do more. In history, when the old man was founding the country and the religious nuts, his Ikhwan, wanted to invade Iraq and he knew that the British did not want him to and would cut off his money he kept them from doing that. He in essence waged a war on his own troops and won. When the royal family chooses to lay down a marker I think they can.

And so I believe that is why I am intrigued with what the young guy is doing when he talks about, and I know talk is cheap, but talks about moderate Islam. The young people in Saudi Arabia these days are not just dependent on Saudi TV. You can now get 90 channels of TV. You can watch anything in Saudi Arabia. And they are all on the internet and they all do have a much greater idea about what goes on in the rest of the world.

So there is some change in the society, and I remind you again 70 percent of the people are under 30 years of age. It could be a quite different Saudi Arabia not liberal like this country, but it could be a quite different place in 10 years if the society cut off from its ability to be passive and dependent on the government through spending oil to give everybody a job and buy their loyalty which they can't afford anymore, if people become self-reliant which they are urging them to do—we have to see if this transpires—it will be, I think, a somewhat different society.

Mr. POE. I thank the witness. Mr. Rohrabacher from California.

Mr. ROHRABACHER. Thank you very much. We were talking about words, a little back and forth on words. Let me just note, sometimes it is discouraging to hear people use certain words or the inability of certain people to use words. At a time when radical Islamic terrorism threatens to murder tens of thousands, if not more, Americans, it is quite disconcerting that our own President can't use the term ''radical Islamic terrorism.'' And that needs to be looked at closely.

In terms of the Saudis, I will have to suggest that Ms. House that I like your optimism, but there is a thing called irrational optimism. And that is when someone gets beaten in the head a number of times and think they can do the same exact thing without getting beat in the head. The Saudis have been financing terrorism now for 20 years at least, at least. I mean they are, Saudis were behind the Taliban. Saudis financed Pakistan and they still do, and the Taliban were financed by that money.

Just what, 2 days ago there was a drone attack where we took out the new leader of the Taliban, and where was he? He was in Pakistan. And who do you think is paying his bills in Pakistan, the Pakistanis? They are broke. They get their money from Saudi Arabia. So the Saudis have been financing this mayhem.

I mean, it is not just the fact that 15 of 19 of the terrorists that murdered 3,000 Americans on 9/11 that they were Saudis, but it is what the government has actually done. And let me ask, how many of you there believe that the royal family of Saudi Arabia did not know and was unaware that there was a terrorist plot being implemented that would result in an historic terrorist attack in the United States in the lead up to 9/11? Do you believe that the Saudi royal family did not know? Raise your hand if you think that.

Oh, okay. Let me just suggest this, that—okay. We have two and two, I think. So you guys believe that the Saudi royal family may well have known there was a major terrorist attack coming.

Mr. ROEMER. Mr.——

Mr. ROHRABACHER. Go right ahead.

Mr. ROEMER [continuing]. Congressman, you and I go way back from our time together when I served up here. That is just too difficult of a question for somebody to raise their hand or put their hand down to——

Mr. ROHRABACHER. Well, it is not for me. I will raise my hand right here. And let me tell you something——

Mr. ROEMER. Have you read the 28 pages?

Mr. ROHRABACHER [continuing]. That within 4 months before 9/11, I was tipped off by a very high ranking Taliban who happened to work with me in Afghanistan when we were fighting the Soviets that there was going to be, there is a plot going on and what do you think about this ongoing plot? And I might say, the Warren Commission didn't seem to—when I sent that information over that I had been tipped off, they did not follow through on it. I wonder, why?

And so what we have here is a high level ranking member of the Taliban knows about this, but we don't think that the high ranking people in Saudi Arabia who are financing the whole thing didn't know about it? This is clear that the Saudis have been intentionally involved in the mass slaughter of Americans and other people in the world in a terrorist way.

We know that they are, number one, we know that they are currently financing madrassa schools and they teach, what do they teach these kids at school? When they come out of them they can, yes, they can be radical Islamic terrorists, but they can't do anything else in the modern economy. They finance mosques that are preaching the worst kind of hatred. And we are hearing about this all the time in the Balkans where they are financing the worst kind of—and we have of course the direct finance of terrorism that we have seen directly into Saudi Arabia.

And we are being told by you today that we really don't know if the Saudi royal family is involved in this. Well, even if they are aware of this they are responsible. After 9/11—they didn't want to kill 3,000 Americans on 9/11. They wanted to kill 50,000 Americans on 9/11. 50,000. That is what they thought. When those buildings were going to come down, they didn't know that we could get all the people out. They were there for a mass slaughter of Americans.

And we have just managed to just sort of, well, let's give them the benefit of the doubt whether or not the royal family knew about this or not. I say that the Saudi royal family has made itself clear that they do not deserve the benefit of the doubt because of all of their actions they have been involved in.

And whether or not the young Saudi royal family members that are watching TV now are going to have an epiphany that Wahhabism isn't really, doesn't demand them to go out and attack the West, whether or not that is going to happen or not I don't think we can rely on that. Especially when you find that all of these young Islamic terrorists are springing up in different parts of the world including in San Bernardino, including at the Boston Marathon, you have these people who have been exposed to Western society but they have also been treated to a very high dose of Wahhabi radical Islamic philosophy that leads them to commit these terrorist acts.

It is either we are going to face reality or there is going to be more and more of our people slaughtered. And I think how we deal with Saudi Arabia it has either got to be realistic or our people are going to suffer the consequences. Thank you, Mr. Chairman.

Mr. POE. I thank the gentleman from California. I thank all of the witnesses for being here. I want to thank the guests in the gallery as well, and also want to recognize some of the folks from the families of 9/11 that are here today as well.

Thank you once again, and there may be other questions we have. You know the routine. We put them in writing, we send them to you, and we expect an answer in 10 days. The subcommittee is adjourned.

[Whereupon, at 4:17 p.m., the subcommittee was adjourned.]

A P P E N D I X

Material Submitted for the Record

SUBCOMMITTEE HEARING NOTICE
COMMITTEE ON FOREIGN AFFAIRS
U.S. HOUSE OF REPRESENTATIVES
WASHINGTON, DC 20515-6128

Subcommittee on Terrorism, Nonproliferation, and Trade
Ted Poe (R-TX), Chairman

TO: MEMBERS OF THE COMMITTEE ON FOREIGN AFFAIRS

You are respectfully requested to attend an OPEN hearing of the Committee on Foreign Affairs, to be held by the Subcommittee on Terrorism, Nonproliferation, and Trade in Room 2172 of the Rayburn House Office Building (and available live on the Committee website at http://www.ForeignAffairs.house.gov):

DATE: Tuesday, May 24, 2016

TIME: 2:00 p.m.

SUBJECT: The U.S.-Saudi Arabia Counterterrorism Relationship

WITNESSES: The Honorable Tim Roemer, Ph.D.
(Former 9/11 Commissioner)

Mr. Simon Henderson
Director
Gulf and Energy Policy Program
The Washington Institute for Near East Policy

Ms. Karen Elliot House
Senior Fellow
Belfer Center for Science and International Affairs
Harvard University

Daniel L. Byman, Ph.D.
Professor
Edmund A. Walsh School of Foreign Service
Georgetown University

By Direction of the Chairman

The Committee on Foreign Affairs seeks to make its facilities accessible to persons with disabilities. If you are in need of special accommodations, please call 202/225-5021 at least four business days in advance of the event, whenever practicable. Questions with regard to special accommodations in general (including availability of Committee materials in alternative formats and assistive listening devices) may be directed to the Committee.

COMMITTEE ON FOREIGN AFFAIRS

MINUTES OF SUBCOMMITTEE ON _____*Terrorism, Nonproliferation, and Trade*_____ HEARING

Day___*Tuesday*___ Date___*May 24, 2016*___ Room_____*2172*_____

Starting Time ___*2:52 p.m.*___ Ending Time ___*4:25 p.m.*___

Recesses _____ (____to ____)(____to ____)(____to ____)(____to ____)(____to ____)(____to ____)

Presiding Member(s)

Chairman Ted Poe

Check all of the following that apply:

Open Session ☑
Executive (closed) Session ☐
Televised ☑

Electronically Recorded (taped) ☑
Stenographic Record ☑

TITLE OF HEARING:

"The U.S.-Saudi Arabia Counterterrorism Relationship"

SUBCOMMITTEE MEMBERS PRESENT:

Reps. Poe, Wilson, Issa, Perry, Zeldin, Keating, Sherman

NON-SUBCOMMITTEE MEMBERS PRESENT: *(Mark with an * if they are not members of full committee.)*

Rep. Rohrabacher

HEARING WITNESSES: Same as meeting notice attached? Yes ☑ No ☐
(If "no", please list below and include title, agency, department, or organization)

STATEMENTS FOR THE RECORD: *(List any statements submitted for the record.)*

TIME SCHEDULED TO RECONVENE _____
or
TIME ADJOURNED ___*4:25 p.m.*___

_____
Subcommittee Staff Director

www.ingramcontent.com/pod-product-compliance
Lightning Source LLC
Chambersburg PA
CBHW081752280526
45789CB00008B/2826